Origen

His Life and Teachings

Origen

His Life and Teachings

By
Fr Tadros Jacob Malaty
Dr. Mina Medhat Shafik

ST SHENOUDA PRESS
SYDNEY, AUSTRALIA
2025

Origen: His Life and Teachings

By: Fr Tadros Jacob Malaty
     Dr Mina Medhat Shafik

COPYRIGHT © 2025
St. Shenouda Press

All rights reserved. Except for brief quotations in critical publications or reviews, no part of this book may be reproduced in any manner without prior written permission from the publisher.

ST SHENOUDA PRESS
8419 Putty Rd,
Putty, NSW, 2330
Sydney, Australia

www.stshenoudapress.com

ISBN : 978-1-7638415-2-9

All scripture quotations, unless otherwise indicated, are taken from the New King James Version®. Copyright © 1982 by Thomas Nelson, Inc. Used by permission. All rights reserved.

Table of Contents

1. Origen and his disciple Saint Gregory the Wonderworker 1
2. The Holy Bible 7
3. Origen and Theologies 15
4. Origen and the knowledge of God 23
5. Origen and Philosophy 33
6. The Faith of Origen and Faith 41
7. Origen and Trinitarian Faith 47
8. Origen and the Love of God 55
9. Origen and Divine Providence 63
10. Origen and the Divine Grace 69
11. Origen and God the Father 81
12. Origen and Jesus Christ 87
13. Origen and the Holy Spirit 141
14. Introduction to Creation 149
15. Origen and Creation 153
16. Origen and the Angels 159
17. Origen and the demons 179
18. Origen and the tolerance of sins 185

19. Origen and the Ecclesiastical Man 189
20. Origen and Martyrdom 219
21. Origen and Christian Worship 233
22. The sign of Origen and the Holy Eucharist 239
23. The Significance of Origen and Baptism 243

1

ORIGEN AND HIS DISCIPLE SAINT GREGORY THE WONDERWORKER

Long before the release of the second volume on the School of Alexandria in English in 1995, I enjoyed the commentaries and annotations of Origen on texts from the Holy Bible. Chapter four of the volume was dedicated to discussing Origen and Origenism.[1][2]

Many Western biblical scholars refer to Origen as the "Prince of Biblical Interpreters," and the University of Oxford in England used to hold a conference every four years to study his personality, writings, and ideas. Some wonder: why doesn't the Coptic Church reconsider the issue of Origen's excommunication? His Holiness Pope Shenouda III answered, saying: Let us not forget that saints who had their fame in the early ages loved this teacher and defended him vigorously during his service and afterwards. At the same time, there were other saints, especially some monks, who accused him of heresy. Some would even

---

1 Fr. Tadros Y. Malaty: The School of Alexandria, Book 2, Origen, 1995.
2 Origen.p197-302.

burn manuscripts they found in a monk's cell. How can we take a different stance after about eighteen centuries?!

What motivated those who could not bear his name in his time?!

1. I previously mentioned that Origen declared that some statements found in his manuscripts and writings were not his words, such as the talk about the repentance of demons, which his opponents inserted to label him as a heretic.

2. Incorrect texts appeared in his book "On First Principles," which some published before he could review it, especially since some of these phrases had not been studied or accepted or rejected by the Church.

3. Origen called on scholars to read everything written and not judge the validity of what is written without reading and examining it carefully.

4. Some did not understand the reason behind his openness to philosophers. At the same time, Origen emphasized the necessity of turning to God, and we must not rely on human opinions without verifying their accuracy.

5. The stance of the Alexandrian Pope Demetrius towards him was due to his preaching in Palestine and Israel in the presence of bishops, which was not allowed in the Church of Alexandria at that time.

6. His acceptance of the priesthood degree from a bishop other than the Patriarch of Alexandria had a negative impact on many.

7. Some believe that his genius in writing was not recognized by many in his time.

What are the concepts of the theologian Origen for religious, preaching, and gospel thought?

Saint Gregory the Wonderworker sent a letter to his beloved teacher, the theologian Origen, who was the new bishop of Caesarea in the third century. It was translated into Arabic by Makarios Jubour and Natasha Yazji from French and Italian, with a review on the Greek text. I felt the need to study this letter, which was published by Nour Publications in Lebanon in the year 2000. I hope it will be a source of support for us in our spiritual life as priests, in our pastoral work, in our understanding of the Holy Scriptures, and will also benefit the servants of the church education, fathers, and mothers in raising their sons and daughters. Here are some of the ideas that were mentioned in this work:

1. The theologian Origen's interest in inner life.

2. Revealing the ease of reaching heaven.

3. Requesting not to focus on one virtue at the expense of other virtues.

4. Emphasizing the necessity of enjoying growth in the knowledge of God and divine mercy.

5. Warning against the beliefs of atheists who ignored the work of divine power.

Excerpts from what Saint Gregory wrote about his teacher Origen3

† He is the angel of the Lord, who has been watching over this saint since my childhood [41].

† This angel disciplined me in his own way, and took good care of me in all circumstances without exception [44].

† When I was a young child who did not understand, and was under the authority of a pagan father, I did not have the opportunity to be his disciple [50].

† Without my will, the divine teacher (Origen) came to my rescue [57].

† We welcomed this man from the very first day, and indeed that day was more important to me than all the previous days. For the first time, the true sun shone upon me [73].

† He kept us close to him through his words, and by the power of divine force [80].

† Perhaps more than all the men of his time, he was a partner with the teacher of piety, the saving Word (divine) [82].

† He listened with his gentle words, and his methods imbued with intellectual emotions [100].

† He taught us not to be content with appearances... but to search meticulously into the essence of things [105].

† Anyone who speaks on a certain topic must strive not to beat around the bush in their speech [108].

---

3   Adapted from Al-Nour Publications in Lebanon:'A Letter to the Teacher Origen, authored by our venerable father among the saints, Gregory the Wonderworker, Bishop of Caesarea.

† In short, we made it possible to enter the sky through this knowledge and that [114].

† We wanted to be organized, balanced, blessed, and truly similar to God [116].

† He urged us most to work, complementing that with actions more than words [126].

† I mean he presented himself as an example of life [135].

† These virtues are very great and noble and cannot be achieved by anyone unless God instills strength in them [146].

† We learned from this wonderful, friendly, and virtuous man to love virtues with extreme love. This is the only thing he could do [147].

† Like the living example, he instilled in us the love of beautiful justice, showing its radiant face like gold, and the love of intelligence that everyone calls for, and the love of true wisdom that is beloved, and the love of divine moderation that is the purity of the soul and peace for all who possess it, and the love of total magnificent power [148].

† I believe our ultimate goal lies in resembling God with the purity of the mind, and getting closer to Him, and dwelling in Him [149].

† Do not fall into the danger of listening to the word of this or that philosopher only, and therefore judging it to be true, even if it never was, and even if it sneaked into our souls deceitfully, and melted in a convincing manner, it will not be able to penetrate us so that we become like wool dyed with an indelible dye [154].

† He advised us not to cling to any philosopher, but only to God and His prophets we should cling [173].

† He is the Creator, guiding and inspiring every prophecy, making His friends the prophets interpreters of every divine word [171].

† The divine word in its interpretation of riddles opens to us what is closed [180].

† This man received from God the greatest gift... He is an interpreter of God's words to humans, understanding matters from God, as if He is speaking to him, and explaining them to humans to make it easier for them to understand [181].

† In one word, you were in paradise (in the words of Origen), as if in the great paradise of God, where we do not have to work for this earth, or to feed our burdened bodies, but we develop spiritual experiences to live happily [183].

2

THE HOLY BIBLE[4]

Origen and the Holy Bible.

Origen told his disciple Gregory that education is beneficial, and that the Bible is the optimal key. Be diligent in reading it, knock and the doorkeeper will open for you. Do not be content with just knocking and investigating, for prayer is the most important thing for reaching spiritual truth. Therefore, he said: "Seek and you will find" (Matt 7:7; Luke 11:9). The Bible is the royal road to knowing God, through it our knowledge is sanctified and transformed into true wisdom.

The Book of the Church

There is no true understanding of the Bible except in the Church, which derives its teaching material from the prophets, the Gospels, and the writings of the apostles. It is the decisive method for doctrine. Origen sees that the true disciple of Jesus receives the key to the sacred scriptures from the traditions of the Church, as well as from the Lord

---

[4] *Fr. Tadros Malaty p 155*

personally. In his interpretation of the sacred scriptures, Origen refers to traditions and writings of the Church fathers. Regarding the parable of the Good Samaritan (Luke 33:10): "One of the fathers said that the man going to Jericho is Adam, and Jerusalem is paradise, and Jericho is the world. And the thieves are the forces of evil. But the Samaritan is Christ. We need to receive the word from the hands of our Lord Jesus."

Origen spent most of his evenings studying the Bible. Saint Gregory said about him: [The inspiring Spirit of the prophets honored him, magnified him as a friend, and made him an interpreter. He had the ability to listen to the Lord, understand what He addressed to him, and then explain it to the people.] His principle in interpretation was: "Explain the Gospel with the Gospel", meaning explaining obscure passages through passages found in the Bible. We need to rely on God in prayer to understand the Bible in its deep meaning.

Symbolic Interpretation

Origen followed a tripartite classification in interpreting the texts of the Bible, including the simple historical meaning, the symbolic meaning, and the spiritual meaning.

Saint Clement and Origen resorted to interpreting the anthropomorphism of the divine (i.e. attributing human qualities to God) as symbols of His actions and power. The Gospel often speaks of God as if He has human limbs like hands, feet, eyes, ears, mouth, etc. and human emotions like anger and regret, because God condescends with His love and uses our human language for us to understand Him as we do with our young children when we speak to them in their simple manner.

Origen decides that the Holy Scriptures have a body, soul, and spirit. Its literal or historical meaning represents its body, while its spiritual meaning represents its soul and spirit. The simple-minded find enlightenment through the literal meaning, that is, the direct historical or material meaning. Those at a higher level find enlightenment in the symbolic meaning. And those at the highest level of knowledge receive enlightenment through the spiritual meaning, which contains the shadow of promised heavenly blessings. Origen focused on spiritual interpretation to experience the pledge of heaven in his life.

Many scholars clarify that his theory does not imply a belief in three layers in the church, but rather three stages, each member of which is required to ascend from one stage to a higher one. Thus, Origen does not think in a hierarchical manner. Instead, he seeks an ascending path through three stages of development.

Reaching the vision through the Holy Scriptures

Humans enjoyed the word of God through the prophets and the Lawgiver, and it was covered with letters. The letter truly serves as the body, while the hidden spiritual meaning is realized within it. Therefore, the psalmist says, "Open my eyes that I may see wonderful things in your law" (Psalm 119:18). Who can break the seals of the book that John saw in Patmos, the book written inside and out? No one could open the scroll and break its seven seals, except the Lion of the tribe of Judah, the root of David (Rev 5:5). Our Lord Jesus opens this book and no one can close it. He closes it and no one can open it. The written word is an expression of its spiritual meaning, the work of the Holy Spirit who inspires the writer and the reader. The Holy Spirit is the hidden author of the divine book.

Harmony between the Old and New Covenants

The beliefs in both the Old and New Testaments share a kind of musical harmony between the two covenants. Saint Augustine said: "The New Testament is hidden in the Old Testament. And the New Testament reveals the Old Testament." In one of Origen's writings on the Song of Songs, he explained the relationship between the Law in the Old Testament and the Gospel in the New Testament, saying just as the Law was a prelude to the Gospel, so too was the latter, symbolizing the eternal good news. The Old Testament is an image of the New.

And through it, and in a similar way, it is an image of the Gospel. Just as the Law contains a shadow of the beautiful things to come, and is manifested in the Law that proclaims the truth, so it is with the Gospel, which proclaims a shadow of the mysteries of Christ. As for the eternal spiritual good news spoken of by John, it presents what relates to the Son of God, and the mysteries revealed by His teachings, which represent symbols of their truth.

Origen sees those who shared in the land inherited by the Jews as shadows of those who enjoy paradise. They enjoyed earthly Jerusalem and the temple and the priests... But when our God Jesus Christ came, born on earth, the hour came when the true worshippers worship the Father in spirit and truth (John 4:24). In the presence of truth, the shadow ends, and when the womb of the Virgin Mary became a temple by the Holy Spirit and the power of the Most High (Luke 1:35), the stone temple building disappeared. Here we see the harmony of the patterns of the Old and New Covenants.

Our Lord Jesus Christ, the One, appeared, and with Him Moses, the recipient of the Law, and Elijah, the recipient of prophecy, spoke with Him (Matthew 17:3). And when Peter, James, and John lifted up their eyes, they saw Jesus standing alone, and no one else was with Him. They became one with Jesus (the Gospel). And everything had changed: they were not three, but our Lord Jesus Christ alone, to confirm that the goal of the two covenants is to enjoy the Lord Jesus Christ, the Savior of the world.

The Holy Bible and the Pure Springs.

Origen believes that the wells dug by Abraham's slaves were filled in by the Palestinians after his death, so neither Isaac and his people nor the Palestinians benefited from them, indicating a literal interpretation of the Law. No one was allowed to drink from the Gospels, but they suffered "from thirst for the word of the Lord" until Isaac came and dug the wells of water anew for them to drink. We give thanks to Jesus

Christ, the Son of David, the Son of Abraham (Matt 1:1), who came and opened the wells for us. We say with the disciples of Emmaus: "Were not our hearts burning within us while he talked with us on the road and opened the Scriptures to us?" (Luke 24:32). Thus Origen showed that this great impact of Christ's teachings was prophesied in the Old Testament scriptures.

The Sweetness of Spiritual Interpretation

Origen says: I believe that the Law was bitter. For the weak child suffered from the wound of circumcision on the eighth day as prescribed in the Law, but those who are "born of the Spirit" "in water" (Matt 3:11; John 3:5) cannot taste the bitterness of circumcision, but enjoy the eternal heavenly wedding feast.

Preparation to Hear the Word of the Lord

Origen warns us against hasty reading of the books of the Holy Scriptures, which prevents us from gaining depth, as we must prepare ourselves to follow Hosea who says: "Yet the number of the children of Israel shall be as the sand of the sea, which cannot be measured or numbered. And it shall come to pass in the place where it was said to them, 'You are not My people,' there it shall be said to them, 'You are sons of the living God.' Then the children of Judah and the children of Israel shall be gathered together, and appoint for themselves one head, and they shall come up out of the land, for great will be the day of Jezreel" (Hosea 1:10-11). He asks us to do everything possible so that the Lord may grant us the grace to understand the Holy Scriptures. And we ask the Lord to increase the word within us, so that we may take abundance from the breadth of the horizon in Jesus Christ, and be able to hear the sacred words.

If you dedicate your life to meditating on the law of the Lord through the spirit of wisdom, the "heart" that meditates on the law of the Lord will take over, and it has the power to break down great cities and fortresses, meaning it shatters the words of the liars, and becomes worthy of the blessing of Hosea. If anyone gathers to hear the word of the Lord, let him hear what the Lord commands. After purifying himself, he must listen to the word, and he must wash his garments. For he who comes with dirty clothes to this place hears: "Friend, how did you come in here without a wedding garment?" (Matt 22:12). Therefore, no one can hear the word of the Lord unless purified, that is, "holy in body and spirit" (1 Cor 7:34), meaning washing his garments. Then he goes to the wedding feast, eats of the Lamb's body, and drinks from the cup of salvation.

When Rebekah, whose name means patience, saw the servant and meditated on the prophetic word "she let down her pitcher upon her hand" (Gen 24:18), because she spoke a simple prophetic word: "Drink, and I will water your camels" (Gen 24:14). So the soul that works with patience and longs to learn, and is accustomed to draw knowledge from the depths and unite in heavenly marriage with Christ, if she comes to the wells every day, drinks the water and waters others, and thirsts for the word of the Lord.

We must read with pure hearts because "no one can hear the word of the Lord, unless he is holy in body and soul, no one enters this wedding with torn garments."

The word of the Lord and betrayal

Origen believes that those who ate the heavenly manna in faith tasted its sweetness, while those who did not eat it, but hid it, it generated worms and stank (Exod 16:20), even those who accepted the word of the Lord in betrayal and did not eat it, for its sweetness turns into worms.

The word of the Lord is within us.

The book says: "But what does it say: "The word is near you, in your mouth and in your heart," that is, the word of faith which we preach. Because if you confess with your mouth the Lord Jesus and believe in your heart that God has raised Him from the dead, you will be saved" (Romans 10:8-9). When "you believe in your heart," your heart and understanding become gold. And if you confess the word, you will present the confession word as a pledge. For this reason, Moses, who is the spiritual law, says: You take these things from yourselves. They are inside you. Even if you are poor, you can still obtain these things. But he emphasizes that each one understands in his heart." Because you cannot offer anything to the Lord from your mouth or understanding of the word unless you understand in your heart what is written. And if you are not alert and listen diligently, the gold or silver will not be complete, because it was required to be purified first. And we hear the scripture saying: "The word of the Lord is pure, like silver that has been refined in a furnace, purified seven times" (Psalm 11:7). So if you understand that what is written in your heart, your gold will be your immense understanding, and your silver, which is the word, will be supreme.

The word of the Lord and union with Him

Surely, this union of the soul with the word can only come through guidance in the divine scriptures, metaphorically called wells. And if one comes to these wells and takes from these waters, it means that by contemplating these words, he finds the deeper meaning, finds a marriage fitting for the Lord, because the soul is united with the Lord.

The word of the Lord and the happy life

Let us also come to pray, to hear the word of the Lord with such faith to see in us that this is the great feast. "Wisdom has built her house, she has set up its seven pillars, she has prepared her meat and mixed her wine; she has also set her table" (Proverbs 9:1-3) which gives us much to find. It is a great feast, as we enter the feast of wisdom, we must not take with us the garments of foolishness, or wrap ourselves in the garments of betrayal, or be stained with the pollution of sin, but simply and with a pure heart, we embrace the word and serve the divine wisdom, which is Jesus Christ.

3

ORIGEN AND THEOLOGIES[5]

What are the circumstances of Origen?

Throughout the early Christian ages, there was no writer who equaled Origen in his attractiveness, his studies, and his glory. Many scholars believe that Origen is the founder of Christian theology. His theologies were influenced by the following factors:

1. *Origen was committed to dealing with three categories: philosophers, heretics, and simple believers.*

The Alexandrians (the School of Alexandria) were preoccupied with philosophy to correct philosophical views that were contrary to faith and to attract knowledgeable individuals to have faith in Christianity.

Origen built his doctrine on his own comments on the Bible and urged Christians to adhere to Christian teachings.

Origen's heart was aflame to attract the world to faith, illuminate the true spiritual Church, advance every soul in divine knowledge and

---

5 *Cf. Fr. Tadros Y. Malaty: Origen, 1995, page 289-302.*

union with the heavenly bridegroom, and engage in continuous praise like the heavenly beings. Therefore, it is not fitting for us to rely solely on his work "On First Principles De Principiis" which he completed in his youth. His sermons to the simple, bishops, and philosophers had their impact on his theological system and his stance on soteriological theology.

Heresies and heretics in his time

Christianity ran in his blood, and he did not accept any compromise with heretics. While still an orphan at the age of seventeen, he received material support from a wealthy lady who adopted him. This lady was associated with a famous heretic from Alexandria named Paul. No one could convince Origen to join him, as he strongly detested heretics.

First: The main heresy he faced was "Gnosticism" as faced by Saint Irenaeus, Tertullian, and Saint Clement of Alexandria. He discussed it in the first book, chapter four: "The School of Alexandria and the Gnostics," as well as confronting the leaders of the Gnostics, especially the trio of Basilides, Valentinus, and Marcion, regarding the following points: Their system was based on the perpetual antagonism between the "Creator of the material universe" Demiurge, and the being transcendent beyond human knowledge, while Origen insisted on the unity of God the Father and Jesus Christ. The Gnostics distinguished between the old and new covenants, while Origen, like the other Alexandrian fathers, emphasized the fundamental unity between the Creator God in the Old Covenant and the same God orchestrating salvation in the New Covenant.

Some taught that Paul of Samosata, the bishop of Antioch, sits at the right hand of Christ in heaven, and Marcion sits at his left. Marcion viewed the Creator in the Old Covenant as a harsh and vengeful God, not a loving God.

Origen's main decision was to open the list of proposals with the

Law of Faith, at the beginning of his Treatise on First Principles, and in opposition to the Marcionite and Gnostic doctrines, which separated the Creator in the Old Testament from the Father of Jesus Christ. There is only one God for the Law, the prophets, and the apostles. The Lord Jesus came with the purpose of calling Israel, and when Israel rejected him, he also called the nations.

Secondly, he opposed the doctrine of Valentinus, who claimed the existence of three natures for the souls. Therefore, Origen revealed the equality of free will in rational beings, in an equality that is only broken by voluntary action and human freedom that accepts or rejects divinity.

Thirdly, Origen faced two conflicting trends in theologies related to the Trinity:

1. *Those who tried to maintain the absolute unity of God by ignoring the Holy Trinity, or the unity of divinity "monarchy," and considered the "Son" as just a name and external form of the Father. They were called "Noetians" for their affiliation with Noetus in Smyrna and Sabellius from Libya, and later the Sabellians, while in the West they were called Patripassians, for believing that the Father suffered.*

2. *The Adoptionists, who also desired to maintain the "absolute unity of God monarchy," considering that Christ is just a man adopted by God as His son, for his virtues.*

It is possible that there was a blending of these two doctrines. Origen was fully familiar with terms like "Trinity" and "Hypostasis." He believed that the Father, Son, and Holy Spirit are three Hypostases, and he affirmed that each Hypostasis is distinct from eternity, and not just a distinction in administration. This affirmation is one of the main features of his doctrine.

The Heretics and the Path of Faith.

Origen believes that heretics first accept the deposit of faith, then later deviate from it out of pride, and search the Scriptures not to discover the truth, but to confirm their own doctrines. Henri De Lubac says: [One must accept faith in God, in the Spirit taught to us by the Church. And not act like heretics who search the Scriptures just to find what confirms their own doctrines. Their pride elevates them to "higher than the cedars of Lebanon" and their sophistry is filled with deceit, and there is no benefit in their claim to have a tradition that came to them from the apostles, for they are masters of error. While the faithful Christian never strays from the great tradition, they desire to make us worship a "Christ" they invented... while our true Christ reveals Himself "within the house," they distort those vessels of gold and silver, which are the sacred texts, to shape them to fit their desires. They are forgers, laying their doctrines outside the Church. They are teachers of lies and prophets of lies, isolating from their thoughts what they suggest. They are the liars spoken of by Ezekiel, who with their deceitful scheming display their idols - which are their empty doctrines - with sweetness to their listeners, to confirm their deviation. They all claim that Jesus is their teacher and embrace Him. But their kiss is the kiss of Judas.]6

Let it be known to us that the gates of hell have their names according to the type of sin. One gate of hell is called "immorality," through which the immoral pass. Another is called "denial," through which the deniers of God pass to hell, and all heretics and those with "false knowledge" (1 Tim 6:20) who have each established a gate to hell, like Marcion, Basilides, and Valentinus. Satan, the deceitful enemy, offers a stone instead of bread (Luke 11:11). This is what Satan wants, for stones to be turned into bread, so that people may feed on stones that appear as bread. So if you see heretics eating their false teachings like bread, know that their discussions and teachings are like stones, offered by

---

6   Henri De Lubac: Origen, On First Principles, NY., 1966 (Koetschau text together with an introduction and notes by G.W. Butterworth, p. XIV

Satan for us to eat, as if they were bread. Should we beware of eating Satan's bread, thinking it is the bread of the Lord. Satan speaks from the Scriptures and relies on them. May he not deceive me, even if he uses the Scriptures.

The anthropomorphites (and the Alphians and the literalists)

Origen opposes those who are given three designations:

1. The Anthropomorphites, who adhere to anthropomorphism, that is, to literalism and depict God in bodily form. In contrast, Origen affirms the non-bodily nature of the three hypostases, explaining that God is spirit. And alone without a body. Therefore, the Trinity, which is the origin of all things, should not be considered bodily, as it is completely non-physical.

2. The Chiliasts or Millenarians, who believe literally in the thousand years mentioned in the Book of Revelation (20: 1-10). They believe that there will be a first resurrection for the righteous, and they will reign during this time in the heavenly Jerusalem, which will descend to earth, where they will enjoy happiness with Christ before the final resurrection.

   Origen opposes the prevailing resurrection doctrine among the Millenarians. Regarding the state of the body after this resurrection, they imagine it to be identical to the earthly body, to the extent that people will eat, drink, marry, and bear children. And that the heavenly Jerusalem will be like any city here on earth, and that the spiritual body will not differ in any way from the earthly body.

3. The Literalists, who maintain the literal meaning of the written word and reject the spiritual meaning.

Origen's soteriological theology

Origen focuses on the salvation of himself and others in all his works. His heart was aflame with the desire to renew souls and glorify them through the redemptive work of the Savior of the whole world.

1. Origen's patterns related to theology, spirituality, ecclesiology, angelology, and eschatology, etc., are all directed towards the return of the rational creation to its eternal rest. This cannot be achieved through personal effort, especially for humans, who need divine grace to enjoy the work of the saving Redeemer.

2. Origen, as a disciple of Clement of Alexandria, faced Hellenistic (Greek) culture not for attack, but to affirm that salvation is practical philosophy. Jesus Christ, the Savior of the world, came to enlighten and teach us. He is the light of the world, who rescues us from the darkness of ignorance, and grants us victory over the demons who obscure the light of truth from us. Christ is the heavenly teacher who renews our nature with His Holy Spirit, and raises us with Him to His heavens - the chamber of His wedding - where the Word of God (John 1:1) reveals His divine mysteries to His bride.

Origen gathers in one place all the titles he finds in the Bible that express the nature of the work of Christ as the Savior of the world. He explains that these titles are for our satisfaction, life, justification, salvation, and glorification. He is the light of the world (John 8:12), the way, the truth, and the life (John 14:6), the resurrection (John 11:25), the door (John 10:9), the good shepherd (John 10:11), the Alpha and the Omega, the beginning and the end, the first and the last (Revelation 22:13), the Messiah who is called Christ (John 4:25), the Word, and God (John 1:1), the Son of God the Savior, the power of God (Romans 1:16), the righteousness, holiness, and redemption (1 Corinthians 1:30), the king, the teacher, the Lord, the true vine and the living bread, the sword, the servant, the burden of God, the Paraclete, the atonement, the wisdom, the sanctification, the creator, and the high priest. Origen derived these ideas in the context of his discussions on the salvific work of Christ, in his sermons.

Young M. Frances states that all interpreters of Origen's thought consider Christ as a teacher and giver of enlightenment, that is, the Word of God, as his distinctive view of the salvific work of Christ. It is not surprising that this is the main statement of Origen about the salvific work of Christ in De Principiis, considering that this work was dominated by philosophical issues and ideas. This is also highlighted in "Commentary on John."

Faith in the Holy Trinity and Aaron's dry rod that budded

In the commentary on the Book of Numbers (17:8) regarding the budding of Aaron's rod, Origen says: [Everyone who believes in Christ dies first and then is born again. This is another lesson in the budding of the dry rod. The first branch of it is the first confession of man in Christ. Then the leaves come when the newborn receives the gift of grace from sanctification by the Spirit of God. And then he bears flowers, when he begins to make progress as he receives the grace of purifying qualities, presenting flowers of mercy and righteousness. Finally, he presents the fruits of righteousness, which the believer not only lives by, but also gives life to others. When he reaches perfection, he spreads the word of faith, as the presence of fruits that nourish others. This is the manner in which the diverse kinds of believers possess the rod of Aaron, which is a symbol of Christ.]

4

ORIGEN AND THE KNOWLEDGE OF GOD[7]

Knowledge as confirmation of salvation.

Men of the school of Alexandria were preoccupied with "knowing God", so for them this knowledge is enjoying union with the Father in the only Son by the Holy Spirit. Through the true practical knowledge of the Holy Trinity, we enjoy the life established in Christ, by the work of the Holy Spirit in us, instead of the spiritual death we suffered because of our sins. Knowledge, for Origen, is not just intellectual contemplation of God and His glory, but a daily practice in our worship and life with God, like union with Him and practicing love. Knowledge for Origen is the same as love. Origen relies on the Hebrew meaning of the verb "know", which is used to express the act of human love. Adam knew his wife Eve. This is the absolute definition of knowledge, which is union in love. Just as man and woman are "two in one body", so God and the believer become two "in one spirit".

---

7   CF. Fr. Tadros Y. Malaty: Origen, 1995, page 305.

Henri Crouzel says that knowledge is participation in the goal, and even union with love. The manifestation of the Lord Christ symbolizes the highest knowledge of God in His Son, so our ascent on the mountain with the three apostles Peter, James, and John (Matthew 17:1) symbolizes our daily spiritual ascent. As for those who remain in the plain, they see Jesus "without appearance or beauty" (Isaiah 53:2), even if they believe in His divinity. We conclude from these words (Luke 1:2) that knowledge is a goal in itself, crowned by actions. Just as knowledge is linked to actions, so is knowledge for the service of the Word. Origen considers the grace of knowledge a free gift from divine love, which man must receive with full freedom of will.

Human knowledge and ecclesiastical tradition

Origen places his trust as a churchman in ecclesiastical tradition, as a source of Christian doctrines, with breadth in vision and openness in heart. He believes that the human mind is a divine gift, and is itself an image of divinity. Because the similar is known by its similar, the mind perceives the mind. Origen decides that knowledge of God is not achieved by physical eyes, but by the mind, as it is in the image of the Creator, and by divine providence it gains the ability to know God. There is an intellectual vision that differs in its nature from sensory vision: as much as the high eye is awake and sensory vision is closed, every person perceives the supreme divine essence, and the Son who is the Logos and Wisdom.

The wisdom of God and the wisdom of the world

Origen does not mix between human wisdom and divine wisdom. Human wisdom, which we call "temporal wisdom," is foolishness. As for "divine wisdom," it differs from human wisdom, as it comes as a grace from God, bestowed upon those who prove themselves ready to accept it. It is not strange that some who are interested in arts, sciences, ethical discussions, or literary problem-solving studies are ignorant of God. Their intellectual abilities resemble a human's vision and observation of everything except the sun, as they never raise their gaze towards its rays.

Our progress in knowledge is continuous.

Despite Origen's view of God as light, he sometimes hints at the darkness in which humans hide their selves due to their physical condition. The goal is knowledge "face to face." In the resurrection, we will have knowledge similar to that of the angels, although Origen did not clarify the extent of the perfection of that knowledge.

Knowledge of God

"God" is invisible and beyond expression in words, as what is divine cannot be articulated by humanity (2 Cor 12: 4, Rom 11: 33). Speaking about God is difficult to deal with. Origen decides that God, through His supreme love for us, uses our human language and expressions to communicate with us. "For I, the Lord your God, am a jealous God" (Exod 20: 5). Notice the compassion of God. He adopts human tendencies to teach us and make us complete. Who, upon hearing the phrase "a jealous God," does not feel amazed and think of human weakness? But God does everything for us, even teaching us, speaking in terms familiar and customary to us. Let us contemplate what this statement "I am a jealous God" means. Furthermore, Origen's creed accepts what is said about God without reservation, rejecting traditional Platonic definitions that God is unchanging, impassible, without form or color, not in need of the world, even though He created it by His goodness. Despite his talk about not sensing the feelings of the divine Lord, that He has no human emotions, he insists on declaring the true fatherhood that He has - through His love - expressing it in a human manner, as if He had all the feelings and emotions. It was said: "As a man carries his son, so the Lord your God carried you" (Deut 1: 31).

God is incomprehensible.

1. Origen says that the incomprehensible God declares His essence, nature, and attributes for the benefit of humanity. God desires His created beings to know Him, so that they can imitate Him and share in His life. In other words, the establishment of the spiritual Church as the bride of Christ is the true goal of theology, or of our faith and knowledge of God. God is a free and sovereign being, offering Himself to be understood by His creatures, who are characterized by personal perfection, and are expected to have a free will relationship with God. This faith has brought people from the East, West, North, and South together in the knowledge of God.

2. God is immaterial and incomprehensible. However, He reveals Himself to people, especially if their minds are pure. There is a connection between the human mind and God. The mind itself is an image of God. Therefore, it has a concept of the divine nature, especially the purer it is and the further it is from materiality.

3. Plato thought that knowing God is difficult, if not impossible. It is likely that knowledge of God may be beyond the capacity of human nature.

    This explains the serious errors about God among people. But through God's compassion and love for humanity, with a miraculous divine gift to achieve knowledge of God, those whom He foreknew, He also predestined (Romans 8:30), for them to live a life worthy of Him, after He revealed Himself to them.

4. God does not feel pain and harm, yet at the same time, He is not a static being as He is "love," a unique love. We imagine love according to our human nature, so that we can understand and

accept it. Therefore, we read in the Bible that God grieves for our fall into sin, He hates sin, and rejoices in our repentance.

Origen provides many examples of this, then concludes that all these passages, which speak of God grieving, rejoicing, or hating, must be understood as written in a figurative and human style. The divine nature is far from all emotions of pain and change, remaining eternally steadfast and untroubled, above the peak of its bliss. God is not a part of the created order, but infuses it with life through His existence and power.

Origen began by acknowledging that God is incomprehensible. God can only be understood indirectly, through reasoning from the universe and the created order. Because God is perfect, He created a world of spiritual beings and souls that share in His eternity. Origen believes that God always requires a world that can be attributed to Him. However, this world cannot be considered as a second foundation alongside God.

Knowledge of God and Grace

"No one knows the Father except the Son, and those to whom the Son chooses to reveal him" (Matt 11:27; Luke 10:22). This indicates that God is known through a specific divine grace, which does not come to the soul without His permission, but through a kind of true inspiration. It is likely that knowledge of God is beyond the reach of human nature, which explains the confusion people experience regarding God. However, due to God's favor and love for humanity, and through miraculous divine grace, knowledge of God extends to those who came before and whom God placed in advance of His knowledge, as they are intended to live a life worthy of Him after He revealed Himself to them. Through His love for humanity, God has revealed the truth and all knowledge about Him (Rom 1:18), not only to those who have dedicated themselves to Him, but also to some who know nothing about pure worship.

Inspiration from God

Our Savior is the image of the invisible God. Compared to God Himself, He is the truth that only the Son knows and those whom the Son chooses to reveal Him to. Everyone who believes and is confident that "grace and truth come through Jesus Christ" (John 1:17), and who knows that Christ is the truth, accepting His statement: "I am the way, the truth, and the life" (John 14:6), receives knowledge that encourages people to live a good and happy life only through the words of Christ and His teachings themselves. By the words of Christ, we do not mean only those spoken during His incarnation, for the Word of God existed before that time, in Moses and the prophets.

Beholding God and His Angels

Origen affirms the following truths:

1. God and His angels can only be beheld through a pure heart.

2. This beholding is a divine gift bestowed upon us according to His will. God and His angels are present with us, but we do not see them. Divine grace grants the righteous the vision of God through their inner sight.

3. Even if a person beholds God, they will not see Him as He is.

Origen's statements on the knowledge of God.

❖ Allah appeared to Ibrahim and other saints, through divine grace...

It is possible that there are angels with us now as we speak, but we are unable to see them because we are not deserving of it. Perhaps the physical eye, or the inner eye, seeks to achieve this vision. But if the angel does not reveal himself to us - those who aspire to see him - we will not be able to do so. This fact is not only related to witnessing God in the present time, but also extends to the time when we transition from this world. For God and His angels do not appear to everyone after their transition... but it is a privilege granted only to the pure of heart, who have prepared themselves to witness God. The person burdened with sins is not at the level of the one with a pure heart. The latter will witness God, while the former will be deprived of that.

I believe this is what happened when Christ was incarnate in our world. Not everyone who saw him witnessed him. Pilate and Herod saw him, but they did not witness him as God. Three men came to Ibrahim at noon. And only two came to Lot in the evening (Gen 19:1). Lot could not bear the greatness of the noonday light, unlike Ibrahim who was able to receive the full radiance of that light.[8,9]

❖ Notice that when the Lord came to Ibrahim, he was accompanied by two angels. But when they came to Lot, only the two angels came. What did they say to him?... "We are sent by God to destroy this place" (Gen 19:13). Lot received them, but he did not receive the one who came for salvation. Ibrahim, on the other hand, received the one who came for salvation, in addition to those who intended destruction.[10]

❖ "The Lord blessed Isaac," as the text says, "and he dwelt by the well of Lahai-Roi - which means the well of vision" (Gen 25:11). That was the result of the blessing that God granted Isaac to dwell by the well of "vision." This is a great blessing

---

8 *Cf. Philo QG. 4.30.*
9 *In Gen. hom. 4:1 (Cf. Heine).*
10 *In Gen. hom. 4:1 (Cf. Heine).*

for those who understand it. May God grant me this blessing, so that I become worthy to dwell "by the well of vision."[11]

❖ As for those who only come to church rarely, who rarely draw from the springs of the Holy Scriptures, and who cast aside everything they hear as soon as they leave and get busy with other matters, such a person does not dwell by "the well of vision." Would you like me to tell you about someone who never turns away from "the well of vision"? It is the Apostle Paul, who said: "We all, with unveiled face, beholding as in a mirror the glory of the Lord" (2 Cor 3:18).[12]

❖ The vision of God is not material, but rather mental and spiritual... That is why the Savior was keen on using the correct word when he said, "No one knows the Father except the Son"... and did not say sees. And again, for those who have been granted to see God, he gave them the "spirit of knowledge" and the "spirit of wisdom", so that by the same Spirit they may see God (Isaiah 11:2).[13]

❖ The organ by which we know God is not the physical eye, but the mental eye, as it sees what is similar to the image of the Creator, and acquires through divine providence the ability to know Him.[14]

❖ And now, even if we are deserving of seeing God with our minds and hearts, we do not see Him as He is, but as He becomes for us in terms of His care for us.[15]

---

11 *In Gen. hom. 11:3 (Cf. Heine).*
12 *In Gen. hom. (Cf. Heine).*
13 *Comm. on Song of Songs 3.*
14 *Contra Celsus 7:33.*
15 *Comm. on Matt. 17:19 on 22:1.*

❖ Even if we are deserving of seeing God... we will not see Him as He is, but as He (suits) Himself to us.[16]

God is love

Despite the early Alexandrian theologians speaking of the impossibility of God feeling pain and harm, and of His impossibility of feeling human emotions, they were keen to emphasize His true fatherhood through His love, expressing it through human language, as if He had every feeling and emotion.

Through love, we can acknowledge God

We must realize how many things need to be said about this love. And also, how many great things need to be said about God, as He is in His essence "love". For just as "no one knows the Father except the Son, and whoever the Son desires to reveal Him to"... similarly, because He is called "love", and as "no one knows the thoughts of a man except the spirit of the man within him, so also the thoughts of God, no one knows them except the Spirit of God" (1 Corinthians 2:11). And here, the Paraclete - the Spirit of truth - who proceeds from the Father (John 15:26) searches for souls worthy and capable of receiving the greatness of this love for God, and for those who are pleased to have it revealed to them.

---

16   *Comm. Matt 17. 17ff.*

5

ORIGEN AND PHILOSOPHY

Why did Origen focus on discussing the Church's view of philosophy and philosophers?

In his time, the world considered philosophy to be the first rank in human life, leading societies to progress and advancement. Science and inventions come in second place after philosophy. In our current era, many consider modern philosophy to be next in line after modern inventions. Studying the stance of the scholar Origen on philosophy and contemporary philosophers helps us understand the correct view of science, scientists, and the evolution of society in terms of scientific knowledge without ignoring the importance of philosophy.

Origen was familiar with and admired the works of Numenius of Apamea, a Platonist who lived in the second century AD, with only a few parts of his works remaining. Numenius wondered "Who is Plato but Moses speaking in elegant Greek?" In his work "On the Good," Numenius used both the Old and New Testaments, with a spiritual interpretation to support his views. We can summarize Origen's view of philosophy in the following points:[17]

1. Origen, like Saint Clement of Alexandria, believed that previous philosophies should be put in the service of Christ. His disciple Saint Gregory said that those who despise philosophy cannot be considered pious. Origen praised philosophy and the sciences, comparing philosophy to the gold that the Hebrews took from Egypt, which unfortunately they used to make the golden calf they worshipped (Exodus 32:1-6). Origen studied philosophy not just out of admiration, but to be able to address those with a philosophical background. Indeed, many students of philosophy, including Saint Pantenus, were influenced by him.

2. By adopting Platonic positions, Origen focused on refuting the first principles of Christian Gnosticism. The compatibility between Platonism and the theological needs of Christianity in its struggle against the Gnostics helped explain the extraordinary influence of Platonism on Origen. He understood the importance of Platonism for his understanding of God and God's relationship to the world, as a preparatory system useful in educating Christians knowledgeable in philosophy that existed before them.

3. Philosophy in his view was a servant, and was not allowed to be its mistress. Jaroslav Pelikan says, "One of the major differences between the theologian and the philosopher is that the former considers himself a 'churchman,' that is, a speaker on behalf of the Christian community, while the philosopher is a servant of philosophy." Origen was not like his teacher, the saint Clement, who turned into a philosopher and then to Christianity. He was not sympathetic towards Greek philosophy. He appreciated the

---

17   A philosopher who lived in Apamea in Syria and in Rome, and flourished in the second half of the second century AD.

beauty of the Greek language and praised it, but his interest in style did not contradict the serious nature of his faith message. Origen focused on emphasizing the falsehood and shortcomings of philosophy, out of fear that believers would be deceived by the beauty of philosophical expressions. In his discussion of the walls of Jericho that Joshua destroyed, he compared philosophy to high walls surrounding the world (Joshua 6:20), and we need the Lord Jesus (the Almighty Joshua) to send his priests and messengers to use their silver trumpets (Numbers 10:2; Psalm 98:6) to preach the heavenly teaching, so that the walls of Jericho that were destroyed may collapse. As for the "golden tongue" stolen by Achan son of Carmi (Joshua 7:21), it is the polluted philosophy that appears shiny and deceives believers with its golden tongue. Origen warns us against philosophy, which the pagans misused by mixing their personal errors with the truth, and declared that philosophy is unable to renew our nature.

4. Origen believed that Platonism contains some truths found in the Bible about truth. His goal was for Platonists to move towards Christianity. Plato was, for Origen, the pinnacle of Greek and human thought away from revelation. He always drew inspiration from him, at least in the form presented by Middle Platonism. In the context of his opposition to Celsus' attacks regarding knowledge of God, Celsus cited many texts from Plato. Origen admired some of them and opposed others, based on Christian inspiration. Despite his great admiration for Plato, he maintained his independence from him, and sometimes criticized Plato in matters different from Christian faith.

5. Origen did not belong to any philosophy, but chose what is good in each theory as a Christian and evangelical theologian. He considered Epicureanism the disgrace of philosophy, for its assertion that pleasure is the highest good, which contradicts

the cross of Christ and denies divine providence, seeing it as atheism for rejecting the recognition of the spiritual privileges of man.

6. Origen approaches the Bible with preconceived concepts, most of which govern his philosophical training. Thus, he can be accused of using Greek philosophy in his interpretation of the Bible. The importance of Origen lies in bridging the gap between Christianity and the Greek world, and his ability to present the Gospel in a language understood by his contemporaries, both pagans and Christians who still retain that culture even after accepting the faith. Origen's view was that Christianity is capable of transforming ancient culture and making it fruitful. Origen addressed many philosophical problems, such as human free will, divine providence, and the relationship between God and man.

7. The main goal of studying philosophy for Origen is to establish a Christian philosophy, that is, Christian theology. After destroying the city of thought, the Christian does not leave it in ruins, but rebuilds it in his own way, using the materials that suit him from what remains of the destroyed city. It is the responsibility of the Church to establish a true philosophy instead of false philosophies, that is, theological philosophy, with interpretive, spiritual, and contemplative content. For him, the mind is a participation in the supernatural mind of God. There is a clear distinction between what is natural and what is divine. Origen adheres to what transcends the natural, implicitly containing the natural. There is no need to resort to an incomplete source if complete teaching is available. If God speaks, should not every human voice be silent? The vessels of flesh in Egypt would not be valuable if we look at the heavenly manna in the wilderness. Accordingly, some human philosophies were found to not satisfy the believer with the emergence of Christi-

anity as a fulfilling system for the soul. Philosophy became an inheritance from a fruitful past, used by the present to establish Christian theologies and preserve them. The legacy is accepted, but with reservations.

Ammonius Saccas and Middle Platonism.

Origen studied philosophy under the philosopher Ammonius Saccas (175-242 AD), who was a Platonist. Ammonius was originally a Christian, but later renounced his faith to embrace Greek philosophy. He had no objection to teaching Christians. In addition to Origen, Heraclas, who would later become the bishop of Alexandria, was also one of his students. Ammonius continued teaching in Alexandria for nearly fifty years, from the time of Commodus (192 AD) until his death in 242 AD. It is said that Ammonius Saccas derived his strength from his profession as a porter at the port of Alexandria. After converting to Christianity, he turned to the study of philosophy at an unknown date during the reign of Commodus, but he retained his old profession, hence he was called Saccas, meaning the porter. R. Cadiou confirms that he saw the young Origen, who attended the lectures of Ammonius Saccas for years. It is likely that Ammonius, like other great teachers, exerted his influence on his students by imparting teachings with utmost tranquility, rather than imposing his personal beliefs.

What prompted Origen to follow Platonism?

With his objections to the Stoics and the Gnostics, who believed that the divine essence is material and that knowledge of God is limited by fate, Origen desired to use Platonism to refute their arguments. He found himself compelled to follow Ammonius, Maximus, and the saints Pantenus and Clement who considered the Platonists and Aristotelians as their allies in their attempts to correct the falsehood of Gnostic Stoicism. At this stage, Origen and Plato were in complete agreement in their rejection of Gnosticism. In Origen's Christianity, even in its rejection of Gnosticism, his followers were taught to despise luxury, sex, and attachment to the very life that preoccupies us in this world. While the famous saying of Plato emphasizes the necessity of escaping this life as much as possible to become like God. And as the Apostle Paul says: "Set your minds on things above, not on earthly things" (Colossians 3:2). If Plato complains about the body as a prison where the soul is tightly confined like a shellfish in its shell, Paul wonders who will deliver him from "this body of death" (Romans 7:24).

What were the beliefs of the new Platonists?

The strongest belief was their belief in the ability of the contemplative mind to find answers to all questions except one, which is about God alone. For God is beyond any measure and above reason. He can only be perceived in three forms: as the infinite, the unlimited, and far from thought, shape, and existence... The One and the Good, the source of all love, and the culmination of all the forces of the universe. This is why the work of a good person focuses on his eagerness to belong to the world of ideas more than the world of material.

Origen found a harmony between Platonism and Christianity, in their insistence on divine providence and human freedom. Like the saying of the Apostle Paul: "And we know that in all things God works for the good of those who love him, who have been called according to his purpose" (Romans 8:28), it seems to echo the words of Plato, that all things that come from the gods work together for the good of those who are dear to them.

Origen distinguished between the simple believers, in their acceptance of the Christian faith, and the small elite of spiritual Christians, who seek to know deep matters about God. For Plato, and also for Origen, the intellectual elite is a spiritual elite, as thought is a characteristic of the soul that alone can reach the contemplation of the true being.

Origen and Plotinus

Many scholars have addressed the relationship between the Christian Origen and the pagan Plotinus, in their main ideas, as famous disciples of Ammonius Saccas, who had a significant influence on later theologians and philosophers. Some scholars believe that they did not meet face to face, but rather encountered each other through certain ideas.

From the basics in the ideas of Plotinus and Origen, they are convinced that the human soul belongs to a world of truth perceived by the mind. Each of them began in their own way to describe the means by which this union can be achieved. Each of them openly declares that the ability and power to move and the desire to return to God were planted by God from the beginning in the soul. Both of them decide that it is the individual soul's responsibility to distinguish the latent power within it, and to strive with a living conscience to reach the world of truths perceived by the mind. However, Origen alone - believing in the unstable and changeable nature of the soul - insists in his writings on the soul's inability by itself to achieve and use the divine power implanted within it, to reach a final participation with God. It is important for the soul to recognize its limits, meaning its instability and independence, if it is to return to God for this grace without which salvation is impossible. If it does so, the soul begins to receive divine guidance and personal and individual grace, which directs it through the different stages towards God. All of this is in harmony with the maturity of the soul and its granted ability, for spiritual progress. Through the soul's living effort, and with the help and guidance of the Logos, the soul is able to achieve perfection and be led to union with God. The Logos is the one who begins by providing the soul with the moral strength, with which it can engage in the battle against sin. And as the rational insight increases, and in the context of its progress towards God, it begins to perceive the divine truths that were previously hidden from it.

From the prevailing Platonic imitation, two opinions emerged about salvation, one Christian and the other pagan. What is common between them stems from that imitation. As for their differences, they arise from each one's concept of human nature. Plotinus, like other Platonists, adopted certain elements of that imitation, reinterpreted them, and derived from them a lofty "anthropology". According to Plotinus, man is fundamentally "divine". His true essence, or rational soul, is a member of the universe perceived by reason, a stable divine entity, imperishable and unchangeable, existing before time, enduring in the perceived universe, and in constant participation with the divine. The goal of human existence is to understand these fundamental divinities, and to return through virtue and philosophy to their original and correct connection with the One, and with the divine world. Origen - also a Platonist - differs from Plotinus, precisely in his adaptation of an opinion that relies more on the Gospel, about creation and the imperfection of human nature.

6

THE FAITH OF ORIGEN AND FAITH

The Greatness of Faith

Origen comments on the words of Saint Matthew, regarding the faith of the centurion, "When Jesus heard this, he marveled and said to those who followed him, 'Truly, I tell you, with no one in Israel have I found such faith'" (Matt 8:10). Notice the greatness of this faith in the eyes of our Lord Jesus, who marveled at it. He does not look at anything else of value like faith, but marvels at faith and considers it acceptable to him.

Lack of faith deprives us of God's work in our lives. Origen comments on the words: "And he did not do many mighty works there, because of their unbelief" (Matt 13:58). We learn from this that the works of the Lord operate in those who believe. "For to the one who has, more will be given, and he will have an abundance" (Matt 13:12). As for those who do not believe, it is not just that the works are not done in them, but as Mark wrote, "And he could do no mighty work there" (Mark 6:5). It did not say: he did not want to do, but he could not do, as if the Lord Jesus wants to cooperate with the faith of that believer with whom power is made, this cooperation is hindered by lack of faith.

Look at those who asked him, "Why could we not cast it out?" He said to them, "Because of your little faith" (Matt 17:19-20). He also said to Peter when he began to sink, "O you of little faith, why did you doubt?" (Matt 14:31). And the woman with the issue of blood said to herself, "If I only touch his garment, I will be made well." This touch for healing, the Savior said about it, "Who touched me? For I perceive that power has gone out from me" (Luke 8:45-46). Also, without faith, a person is deprived of the fruits of the Holy Spirit, that is, of virtues.

What is the goal of faith? And what is the connection between faith and knowledge?

The goal of knowledge is to reach the perfection of the soul, for the soul in Origen's mind is transformed into a flame of love, if it confesses the Father and holds fast to him. Knowledge begins with faith in which we are enriched in all speech and all knowledge (1 Cor 1:5). We must strive to preserve the spiritual laws, so that we may enjoy the crown of our growth.

Faith and victory over hostile forces (i.e. demons)

In Origen's commentary on the words, "If you have faith like a mustard seed, you will say to this mountain, 'Move from here to there,' and it will move, and nothing will be impossible for you" (Matt 17:20), the mountains referred to here are the opposing forces that exist in the flood of evil that settles in some souls. When a person has faith that does not deny anything in the Holy Scriptures, and has faith like Abraham, who believed in God and it was credited to him as righteousness, and he had faith like a mustard seed, then if he says to the mountain, meaning to the deaf and mute spirit, "Move" from the tormented person to the abyss, it moves. Let us pay attention to his saying, "But this kind does not go out except by prayer and fasting" (Matt 17:21). By dedicating ourselves to prayer and fasting, the tormented evil spirit is cast out.

Faith and Prayer

According to Origen, faith is like a mother who gives birth to all the fruits of prayer, and without it, a child (meaning the fruit) cannot be born. Just as it is impossible to have children without a wife, it is also impossible to obtain our requests if we do not approach them with faith accompanied by a life lived in a holy manner.

Faith in the Cross

Although salvation and justification have come to the nations through the Cross, for the unbelieving Jews it becomes a cause of destruction and condemnation. It is written: "Behold, this Child is destined for the fall and rising of many in Israel" (Luke 2:34).

Faith and God's Gifts

When we offer gifts to God from our storehouse, we in turn receive gifts from Him. When we offer Him our faith and love, He pours out on us a variety of gifts of the Holy Spirit. God desires to first receive something from us before giving us something from Him, so that His gifts and generosity appear as a pouring out on those who deserve it. The apostle values these gifts, saying: "But the fruit of the Spirit is love, joy, peace, longsuffering, kindness, goodness, faithfulness" (Gal 5:22).

Faith as a Divine Grace

Divine grace bestows faith upon us and nurtures it. The apostle Paul says that among many other things, the gift of faith is given by the Holy Spirit (1 Cor 12:9; Eph 1:29). Origen cites Luke 17:5, "Increase our faith."

Faith and Works

Faith is trust, and it is not purely intellectual, nor just words we utter, but it is expressed through actions, as a response to divine love and redemptive works. Living faith is the faith that works through love. Moses lifted his hands, and the Amalekites were defeated. Lifting hands here symbolizes lifting our works and deeds to God, refraining from base actions, but rather engaging in all works that please God, and elevate towards heaven. He who "stores up for himself treasures in heaven, lifts his hands to where his treasure is" (see Matt 6:20-21). And as he lifts his eyes, he lifts his hands as it is said: "Let my prayer be set before you as incense" (Psalm 141:2). So if we lift our works, and do not lay them on the ground, the Amalekites will be defeated. We must consider that we are accustomed to being judged before divine justice for our faith, as well as our works (see James 2:24), not just for our works, as if our faith is not subject to accountability.

We hope that you listen carefully to what you hear. Do not be content with hearing the words of God in church, but practice them in your homes, and meditate on His law day and night (Psalm 1:2).

Elkanah had two wives: Hannah and Peninnah (1 Samuel 1:2). Elkanah means "possessed by God," he became a father through his second wife, then God opened the womb of the first, Hannah, in response to her prayers, and she became a mother of a son dedicated to God. The name "Peninnah" means "turning point," while "Hannah" means "grace." Whoever wants to become "possessed by God" must marry these two wives. The first one is joined to us through faith (Ephesians 2:8) so we receive the grace of God. The union with Peninnah, meaning transformation, comes afterwards. After the grace of faith, a person can only experience improvement in behavior and transformation in life.

Now, "grace and truth came through Jesus Christ." Therefore, whoever devotes their time to God and the word of God becomes a child of grace. We must be patient to receive our "transformation," first obtaining satisfaction through our holy works. Only then are we entitled to raise a child of grace and receive the gift of the Spirit (Acts 2:38). I mean "Samuel," which means "God is there," for wherever the "spirit of grace" is, there God is present.

7

ORIGEN AND TRINITARIAN FAITH[1]

What is the nature of God our Creator?

The human language cannot express the nature of God. But through His love for humans, He reveals Himself to us, using our human expressions that we use in daily life, as His little children.

God has no equal, for He is the loving Creator who cares for us forever as His beloved creation.

We should not assume that God has a body, but rather He has a rational nature that does not allow for any additions whatsoever.

God is independent of laws, time, and place. He cannot be searched for through human wisdom.

God is unchanging, so why do we offer prayers and sacrifices, as if it is possible for Him to change His decisions towards us? Origen answers that through his prayers, man declares his faith in God and

---

1 *Fr. Tadros Malaty: Origen, page 351 etc.*

his submission to Him. Without divine grace, he cannot acknowledge God, but the word of God declares Him in the Old and New Testaments.

Where is God? And what is the role of His holiness in our lives?

Origen says we cannot comprehend where God is, as He is within us. He is the "light," and as we draw closer to Him, the darkness within us fades away and we enjoy His light. And as we unite with the Logos, we behold the Father face to face, and we are not left without some understanding, even though we do not reach His perfection. We see Him in an unclear form, revealing Himself to us as His rational creation.

"There is no one holy like the Lord" (1 Sam 2:2). No matter how much man grows in holiness, achieving purity and righteousness, it is impossible for him to equal God in His holiness. He bestows holiness upon us and nurtures it, and man accepts it. God is the source of holiness, and man draws it from Him. He is the light of holiness, and man looks upon Him and rejoices.

The Trinitarian faith

Origen is known for his complete understanding of the terms Trias and Hypostaseis and their indications. One of the main features of Origen's doctrine is that the Father, Son, and Holy Spirit are three distinct Hypostases. He affirms that each of them is a distinct Hypostasis from eternity, not just a role in the economy, meaning not limited to their role in salvation history. He adheres to the authentic Trinitarian doctrine, despite using philosophy, he remains committed to the Christian faith. He asserts that the Son and the Holy Spirit are not two powers of the Father, but they are two Hypostases like the Father. By delivering the Holy Trinity through the incarnation of the Logos and the coming of the Holy Spirit, he demonstrates his sense of the unique divinity, known as the Trinity in the New Testament.

The Relationship between the Father, the Son, and the Holy Spirit

Firstly, Origen recognized the importance of the unity of the Son with the Father. He also understood their distinction. He says: [We call Him the Father who is not the Son... and the Son who is not the Father.] The Son's coming forth from the Father is a continuous process, as the Father did not give birth to the Son to send Him away, but He is continuous in His birth and one with Him. Origen's attempts to affirm the unity between the Father and the Son primarily speak of the unity of will and action. In this context, he uses the comparison of marriage, as well as the union between the Logos and the soul. Origen also considers the Logos as an image of the Father or a declaration of divine glory, and he refers to the clarification of the meaning in which two can become one: Adam and Eve were two, but they were one flesh (Gen 2:24). As for the one who is joined to the Lord, he is one spirit with Him (1 Cor 6:17). And Christ says, "I and the Father are one." The unity in the first example is in "flesh," and in the second in "spirit." As for the third example, it is in the one God. Therefore, Origen concludes: "The relationship of our Lord and Savior with the Father and the God of the universe is not like one flesh or one soul, but what is above flesh and soul is the one God." Origen presents the union as being in love and action. He also presents it as an essential union, using the term "homoousios," meaning of the same essence or nature. And he attributes to Pamphilus the famous term homoousion, which the Nicene Fathers used. Origen desires to indicate the distinction between the Father and the Word. He insists that the Son differs in His attributes from the Father, and that they are two. For the Father and the Son differ in their hypostases.

Secondly, the terms hypostaseis and ousia were originally synonymous. The former is Stoic, and the latter is Platonic, and both mean a real essence. Although hypostaseis has this original meaning for Origen, he uses it to mean individual existence. The Son is born from the Father's source. The Logos is always with the Father. Thus, Origen understands that the Logos is God through the coming forth of the Word.

Thirdly: The Son shares in the divinity with the Father. He is the Son of God by nature, and His nature is one with the nature of the Father. This birth cannot be compared to any physical process. He is similar to the emanation of will from the mind. He is the work of the Father's will, a continuous exercise of will, not a solitary act of providence. Origen asserts that the Son is born of the Father, not by a process of division, but in the same manner that will emanates from the mind. Origen affirms that the Logos or Wisdom was begotten apart from any bodily desire, in the same way that will proceeds from the mind. If He is called "the Son of Love" (Colossians 1:13), why not also "the Son of Will"?

❖ *The only Son of God is the Wisdom of God present in His essence, so how can one believe that God the Father existed at any time without the birth of Wisdom? We must believe that Wisdom was without beginning.*

The Son is called "the Logos," as He is the interpreter of the mysteries of the mind of God. His birth is eternal and continuous, like the ray that emanates from the light. He does not become a Son (of the Father) through the adoption of the Spirit, but He is a Son by nature. He alone is a Son by nature, which is why He is called "the only begotten Son." It is necessary to be cautious, fearing the fall into those foolish myths propagated by those who imagine a kind of "elevation" to the divine nature, dividing the fundamental divine existence of God the Father. Indeed, it is the work of the will from the mind without cutting parts of this mind, or separating from it, where the manner in which we think of the Father as begetting the Son can be understood.

❖ *Saint John tells us that "God is light" (1 John 1:5), and Saint Paul calls the Son "the radiance" of the eternal light (Hebrews 1:3). Therefore, since light cannot exist without radiance, how can it be said that there was a time when the Son was not? This is akin to saying that there was a time when there was no truth, no wisdom, and no life! However, we must apologize for using phrases like "there was no time when the Son was not," as these words have a temporary meaning. Nevertheless, if they are used in relation to the Father, Son, and Holy Spirit, they must be understood as indicating something "beyond time."*

Fourthly: The relationship between the Father and His Son, the Word (Logos), is an eternal relationship. It cannot be said that there was a time when He did not exist.

Fifthly: Origen affirmed the consubstantiality of the Holy Spirit, as we will explain in point 11: the Holy Spirit.

Sixth: For Origen, the entire Trinity is involved in the process of creation, in the same way that it participates in the work of salvation. Through the Trinity, the processes of creation and salvation are harmonized. Creation itself serves the purposes of salvation. This is achieved, as it has two distinct levels of truth, helping the soul to choose between spirit and matter, and the good and evil associated with them. To make this choice, human nature must be such that it can be connected to one or the other of these conditions.

The Holy Trinity and the Simplicity of God

Often we are asked this question: How can God have a Son? We answer with another question: Is it not within God's power to have a Son? We cannot accept that God is an inert essence incapable of production. Every active essence must produce something. Fire produces light and heat, radioactive elements produce nuclear energy, and the human mind produces ideas. God cannot be an inert essence, for He has begotten His Son from eternity. He is "the Light" that begets "light". The truth is that the light that does not beget light is darkness. Jesus Christ has been described as "the brightness of His glory and the express image of His essence" (Heb 1:3) and "the image of the invisible God" (Col

1:15), just as the Word is the image of the unseen mind. What can we assume the eternal light, other than God the Father, to be? Was His brightness not with Him (Heb 1:3)? Therefore, there was never a time when the Son was not a Son.

The Unity of the Divine Will

Concerning the unity of the Holy Trinity in the divine will, G. L. Prestige states: [Origen observes that the will of God exists in the will of the Son, and the will of the Son does not deviate from the will of the Father. There are not two wills, but one will, which justifies our Lord's affirmation, "I and the Father are one." He reiterates that the Father and the Son, while objectively distinct, are one in acceptance, harmony, and purpose. Athanasius agrees with Origen in adopting the view that there is one will emanating from the Father and in the Son. Thus, according to this truth, the Son can be seen in the Father, and the Father in the Son. He also says, "Just as God is one in will, so too is He one in activity and power." This doctrine traces back to Athanasius, forming part of his proof of the divinity of the Holy Spirit. He argues extensively that since the Father is the light and the Son is the radiance of Him, the Holy Spirit, as the agent through whom humanity receives its enlightenment, must be perceived in the Son. Therefore, when we are enlightened by the Spirit, it is Christ through whom we are enlightened, as Saint John said: Christ is the true light that enlightens every person. Similarly, the Father is the source, and the Son is the river flowing from this source. However, the Scriptures affirm that we draw from the Spirit, and by drawing from the Spirit, we draw from Christ.

Once again, Christ is the true Son, while through the Spirit, we have become sons and received the spirit of adoption. Therefore, it is concluded that there is a holy and complete Trinity, expressed as the Father, the Son, and the Holy Spirit, containing nothing foreign or derived from an external source, with a cohesive and undivided nature, and a single power. Thus, the Father always works through the Logos in the Holy Spirit. Therefore, the unity of the Holy Trinity is preserved. In the Church, one proclaims one God, who is always, for all things, and in all things. He is always as the Father - as the head and source - and for all things in the Logos, and in all things, that is, in the Holy Spirit.

Unity in Action

In this Trinity, there is no room for claiming who is greater or lesser, or for there to be a separate action. The gift of the Spirit is declared by the Son and operates through the Father. The Father, the Son, and the Holy Spirit are three hypostases and operationally one, in essence and life. Therefore, through the connected action of the Father, the Son, and the Holy Spirit within us - which occurs in successive stages - we attain the holy and blessed life of the saints.

God the Father gives everyone the gift of existence, and makes participation in Christ by virtue of being the Logos or the Mind, making them rational. As a result, they are exposed to praise or blame, so that they are able to embrace virtue or vice. Based on this, the grace of the Holy Spirit is also available, so that those beings, who are not holy in their essence, become holy through participation in this grace. Therefore, they first receive their existence from God the Father, secondly their rational nature from the Logos, and thirdly their holiness from the Holy Spirit, and those who have already been sanctified by the Holy Spirit are able to accept Christ anew as the righteousness of God. Those who qualify to advance to this rank through sanctification by the Holy Spirit receive the gift of wisdom, through the power of the work of the Spirit of God. I believe this is what Paul meant by saying, "To one is given through the Spirit the utterance of wisdom, and to another the utterance of knowledge according to the same Spirit."

8

ORIGEN AND THE LOVE OF GOD[2]

The righteousness of God and His love

Origen asserts that man is the dearest friend of God and the object of His love.

1. The Lord is the shepherd of all souls. He desires the salvation and glorification of human souls. They are like sheep in their weakness and deviation from discipline and reason, and He is their shepherd.

2. The Lord cares for man, by His divine providence He subdues nature and all circumstances for his sake. In his commentary on the crossing of the Red Sea, Origen explains how God subdued nature for the sake of man, and compelled the elements themselves to be subject to your will, even in what is contrary to their nature (Exodus 14:21).

---

2 Fr. Tadros Malaty: Origen, page 366 etc.

3. *God does not want man to be isolated from heaven, so He grants him Himself as a grace to lead him to heaven.*

4. *God declares His love through His salvific work: through the incarnation of the Word of God, His crucifixion, and His resurrection.*

Before discussing divine providence, the free grace of God, and the salvific work of Christ in separate articles, I would like to address Origen's answers to the following questions:

What is the purpose of God's love?

God does not need anyone other than the salvation of His creation in His love. Origen elaborates on the true meaning of "love." And because the Father is the "greatest good," so too the Son asks us to resemble Him, so that through the goodness in Christ Jesus, we are connected to Him as if in a kind of blood relationship.

Why is God said to be jealous?

Allah is jealous, He desires that you be attached to Him, so if He frees you from sin and rebukes or disciplines you, and if He is angry, and if He feels any kind of jealousy towards you, then be sure that there is hope in your salvation. Allah does not desire for a soul that is connected to Him in faith to remain in sin. Rather, He wishes for it to be purified immediately, and to rid itself of all its impurities, if it has been contaminated by some of them. But if the soul continues in its sin and says, "I will not listen to the desire of the Lord, but I will do whatever I want" (Jeremiah 7:18), then it will be under judgment, "Because I called and you refused, I stretched out my hand and no one paid attention, and you neglected all my advice and did not want my rebuke, I will also laugh at your calamity" (Proverbs 1:24-26).

How does God not know sinners?

God loves repentant sinners, those who have sought His mercy, and He alone is able to support them. In his commentary on the Book of Psalms, Origen says that God knows the righteous, and does not know the wicked. It is not fitting for God to know evil, therefore sinners are not in the sight of the Lord. As for the righteous, they are the opposite, they belong to Him, they are His children, the Father knows them through His only begotten Son, who shares alone the knowledge of the Father, and the Father knows them in Him.

How does God turn evil into good for the righteous?

God did not create evil. And if some practice evil, He does not forcibly stop it, despite His ability to do so, but He uses it in accordance with His wisdom. Through the wicked, He makes those who strive for righteousness more illustrious and deserving of mention. If evil disappeared in this world, there would be nothing to stand against righteousness. And then, righteousness would not shine with its great splendor. Righteousness is not righteousness unless it is proven and tested. Also, God does not dwell on earth or in the hearts of the wicked, but the righteous enjoy the pledge of heaven (2 Corinthians 6:16).

Why is the Lord called the God of impossibilities?

The Lord is called the God of impossibilities because He offers to His believers what is impossible for their understanding, matters that they cannot comprehend with human reason. By the will of God, within reach of understanding and with divine grace available limitlessly, it becomes accessible to some through Jesus Christ, and with the help of the Holy Spirit.

What does divine anger and divine punishment mean?

Allah is eternal and unchanging, without human emotions. But the Bible attributes qualities of anger to Him, as a concession to our weaknesses. He is just and righteous, and does not wish for the sinner to perish. The punishment that befalls the wicked is a necessary consequence of sin, not a result of God's emotions. Divine punishment for humans is not driven by revenge, but for the purpose of discipline, correction, and healing. According to Origen, punishment in this world is educational and stems from the goodness of God. Every suffering that befalls the sinner is meant to teach them a lesson. Origen explains that punishment from God is like a father disciplining his son (Proverbs 3:11) in order to instruct him, rebuke his disobedient student strongly out of fear of his destruction.

The anger of God is not wrathful, but rather a necessary measure. It is a method for human well-being, for treating the sick, and for absolving those who have ignored His words. Everything that comes from God is good, and we deserve punishment. God is a doctor, a father, and a teacher who is not harsh, but forgiving. For the Lord is merciful and "wants all people to be saved" (1 Timothy 2:4). God is quick in His mercy, but slow in punishing those who deserve it.

If we sin, we must say, "I acknowledge my sin to you, and I do not hide my iniquity. I said, I will confess my transgressions to the Lord, and you forgave the iniquity of my sin" (Psalm 32:5). If we do this and confess our sins not only to the Lord, but also to those who can heal our wounds and sins, our evils are erased by the Lord. Truly, a Christian must be under a stricter system than the Old Covenant, because Christ died for it. Now let us hear about the ways of forgiveness of sins in the Bible:

First: We receive the sacrament of baptism for the forgiveness of sins.

Second: We receive forgiveness through martyrdom.

Third: We receive forgiveness through acts of mercy.

Fourth: We receive forgiveness by forgiving others.

Fifth: A person receives forgiveness when the sinner turns away from his sinful ways (Isaiah 55:7).

Sixth: We receive forgiveness through the abundance of love.

In addition, there is a seventh, difficult and painful way of forgiveness, forgiveness through repentance when I say, "I am weary with my moaning; every night I flood my bed with tears; I drench my couch with my weeping" (Psalm 6:6).

The regret of God.

In his sermons on Jeremiah, Origen faces the problem of the "repentance of the Lord" in the Old Testament, as in his saying: "It may be that they will listen and turn back, each one from his evil way, so that I may relent concerning the calamity that I intend to bring on them because of their evil deeds" (Jeremiah 26:3; see also Jeremiah 26:13; 42:10). It is difficult to imagine that God "repents" of His plans, especially since He knows the future. He then goes on to explain that God, despite His difference from humans, still resembles them in order to teach His children. Just as we speak to children in their language - we cannot expect children to understand adult discussions, similarly we understand God's actions towards humans. When you hear about the "anger and wrath of God," do not think that God experiences the emotions of anger and wrath. Because when we give threatening looks to children, it is not because we are angry, but for the child's benefit. If we continued to show our love for them and did not try to correct the child, it would not be beneficial. In the same way, it is said that God is angry, but He aims to correct us. When divine providence intervenes in the fabric of human affairs, it takes into account human reason, behavior, and conduct. Just as you address a two-year-old child in a childish manner, you can imagine God's providence towards the human race.

Therefore, the word "repentance" of God does not mean a change in His position, so why use this term? The prophets had to adopt realistic methods in expressing themselves about God, for the simple people, to give them the opportunity to understand their words. We should not attribute to the Lord the changing qualities specific to the human mind, as by doing so we would attribute to the essence of divine providence a change in His dealings with us.

Divine Providence and Trials

Origen viewed trials as suffering and martyrdom, not as evil events, but as gifts bestowed by divine providence upon some believers. Life under divine care is a continuous test, through which correction of the wicked human's path takes place, and the righteous human is given the opportunity to showcase his virtues. The thorn in Paul's flesh was a gift from divine providence to curb his pride.

If someone tells us unwelcome news, what we call evils are inflicted by fathers, teachers, or surgeons when they use their tools for healing, we say they are practicing "evil," even though our expression does not accuse them. In the same manner, it is said that God sends such so-called "evils" to some people for the purpose of correction and purification.

The reality proves that the trials we go through are intended to reveal our true characters and uncover the secret matters in our hearts. At least we should assume that these trials have come to test and evaluate our love for God. "For the Lord your God is testing you to find out whether you love the Lord your God with all your heart and with all your soul" (Deut 13:3). But if you are tested, you will walk after the Lord your God, fear Him, and follow His commandments. You will *listen to His voice and cling to it, as the apostle calls it "growth from God" in it (Col 2:19).*

Faith is tested through experience, if one endures a trial with faith and proves that faith, then another trial will follow. Things will progress from one stage to another, through various experiences in life. It is said that throughout these stages, the pursuit of more virtues takes place. Thus, the scripture is fulfilled: "They go from strength to strength" (Psalm 84:7), meaning from virtue to virtue, until the soul reaches the goal, which is the highest peaks of virtues, crossing the rivers of God, and rightfully receiving the promised inheritance. If the soul is not seasoned with continuous trials, it will be afflicted with weakness and fatigue. Therefore, the principle has been established, that "every offering you bring must be seasoned with salt" (Lev 2:13).

"The lily" in the Song of Songs 2:2, is the flowers of God's grace, gathered from amidst the thorns of the world.

In my opinion, trials give a kind of strength and defense to the soul. Trials are mixed with virtues, to a degree where the completeness of a virtue does not seem possible without them. No one comes to the circle of martyrdom except by divine providence. God uses the martyrdom of believers as a testimony to attract others to the Christian faith.

Let us learn from the greatness of the benefits that result from the persecution of Christians, the greatness of the granted grace, God's support for them, and the abundance of solutions of the Holy Spirit upon them. Divine grace becomes more accessible in its clearest forms when we receive the evil of people. When the peace of God comes upon us, as we endure suffering from them, despite the fact that Moses and Aaron had attained a high position due to their accomplishments, it was not for the glory of God to shine upon them without them facing persecution, trials, and dangers, even reaching the point of death. Likewise, you who listen to me, do not assume that the glory of God can shine upon you if you persist in your laziness and slumber.

God deals with souls, not within the scope of fifty years or so, but over the unlimited eternity, as He has made our human nature in eternity imperishable.

9

ORIGEN AND DIVINE PROVIDENCE[3]

Divine Providence

Some philosophers denied Divine Providence, while others believed in it, but in a narrow sense. The Alexandrians (the Alexandrian school) believed in Divine Providence in its Gospel sense, meaning its inclusiveness of all creation in general, the universe, nations, animals, birds, and especially humans. Divine Providence transcended time and place, as it included humans even before their creation, and continues to care for them on earth. This care will continue even after death in the eternal life, in the coming age. Divine Providence cares for believers and non-believers, rational and irrational creatures. The Lord reveals this with His kindness, merciful compassion, and also with His discipline, including events that may seem pleasant or unpleasant to us. Origen believes that lack of faith alone is destructive and unethical, as it obscures the inner vision of perceived and unperceived Divine

---

3   Fr. Tadros Malaty: Origen, page 382 etc.

Providence. We confess with unwavering certainty that God cares for all things, even the perishable.

What is heaven but the throne of God, and what is earth but His footstool (Matt 5:35), as proclaimed by the Savior Himself. Oh, His power, which fills the entire universe, including the heavens and the earth, as the Lord says (Jer 23:24).

Divine Providence and Our Creation

We are indebted to the compassionate God for the existence of the universe for us humans, and for His continuous care for us, as He brought us into existence from nothing, and for His special love for the human race even before its creation. The credit for our existence goes back to Him, as it is due to the will of the Creator. The existence of rational beings did not arise by nature, but by the grace of their Creator. He endowed us with minds, free movement, and will, preserved by our free will. God granted humans emotions and desires through which they strive and progress towards virtue. In addition, He implanted the sovereignty of reason within them, through which they can discern between what should be done and what should be avoided.

Divine Providence encompasses everything.

His divine care extends to everything, even the number of hairs on his head (Matt 10:30 and Luke 12:7). We must acknowledge that all events, even the simple and ordinary ones, do not happen by coincidence as some may think, but rather by divine care or divine permission. This is not only for the saints, but for all people. This divine care and divine permission extends even to the "two sparrows" sold for a penny (Matt 10:29), whether those sparrows are in the literal or spiritual sense.

Divine care and concern even for animals

God, with his divine care and divine permission, takes care primarily of rational beings. It also includes non-rational beings, which also benefit from what is planned for humans. Since God governs the movement of the heavens and all that is in them, and all that is on the earth and beneath it and in the sea, with his divine skill including our birth, our food, and the growth of various animals and plants, it is foolish for us to close our eyes and not look to God (Isaiah 6:10, Matt 13:15).

Divine care and the Bible

Divine care arranged for the enjoyment of the Bible in order to provide humanity with divine wisdom and enjoy salvation. Everything written was inspired by the Holy Spirit, so that divine care grants humanity wisdom above human wisdom, and spreads the revelation of salvation in all its books, showing the way to heavenly wisdom.

Divine care and the sanctification of man

R. Cadiou says in his book, titled "God, the Friend of Man". Nothing escapes the plan of divine care, even our efforts in resistance. We can say with the apostle that all the work of salvation is from God. God has bestowed upon rational beings the gift of free will, and has shed his enlightenment upon us. He has planted in our souls the seeds of goodness and perfection, and left us the freedom to accept or reject his gifts. Regardless of our limited role, we attribute the credit for our salvation to the mercy of God, who through his righteousness has brought the work to perfection.

There is no holy like God, and no one resembles the Lord in His holiness, as He is the giver of holiness. Therefore, the work of the Father, the giver of all existence, appears more glorious and radiant when every person ascends through participation in Christ to His wisdom, knowledge, and holiness, in order to reach higher levels of progress. Likewise, when every person sanctifies themselves and increases in purity and perfection, through participation in the Holy Spirit, they become worthy of receiving the grace of wisdom and knowledge, so that all marks of pollution and ignorance disappear from them, to receive purity and perfection. And when the life that God has given to each person becomes worthy of the God who aims to make it pure and complete, so that the creature becomes worthy of its Creator. In this way, by the will of God, a person also attains the ability to live forever and endure into eternity. God takes care of the soul of every person so that they become wise and acquire true knowledge.

Divine Care and Inspiration of Truth

Divine care uses all means to reveal the secrets of God. Firstly, through creation, and then through the natural laws that God has granted to humanity. He also speaks to us through our daily lives, so that we may be in touch with Him. He sent us the Law of Moses and His prophets, and finally the Truth Himself came into our world, incarnated and became human, to reveal Himself to us, and to elevate our souls, minds, and inclinations to the embrace of the Father, through the work of His Holy Spirit.

Divine Care and Demons

In the early centuries of Christianity, when the pagan world was in the grip of demons and evil spirits, the question arose: How can we explain the existence of demons having power over people's lives in a world governed by divine care? Origen and other Alexandrian fathers who experienced divine grace answer, saying:

a. People have become children of the devil (John 8:44), and have entered into a close relationship with him, instead of choosing adoption by God and attaining unity with Him. It is our responsibility, not God's responsibility, to choose between God and the devil.

b. Saint Clement of Alexandria and Origen explain that the demonic order seeks to overthrow humanity and push them into slavery to them. But divine care does not leave us without help, but supports us with angels to protect us if we accept their service (Hebrews 1:14), and to lead believers by the hand to the heavenly marriage, if we desire it.

The Alexandrian fathers explain that in our battle with the demons, we are not alone, as the battle is between God and Satan, so we will not be harmed by them, as we are under the protection of the Almighty God, who makes His angels shade us with their protection if we deserve it, so that we do not suffer from the demons. We are not under the control of the demons, but under the care of the Lord of the universe, Jesus Christ, who brings us to Him. Origen decides that the good angels are more powerful and able to defend us against our enemy. When a person is fortified by faith, Christ entrusts him and sends him a holy angel. "For He will command His angels concerning you to guard you in all your ways" (Psalm 91:11), as the righteous need the help of God's angels so that they are not tripped by the demons and not pierced by an arrow in the darkness.

There are angels responsible for sacred works, guiding to the understanding of eternal light, and to the knowledge of God's mysteries and divinity. Angels are also messengers. Now, if there are those who have been honored with the service of preaching, and if Christ brings good things to His children and preaches the poor with the Gospel, then surely His angels, who are made winds and flaming fire (Psalm 104:4), are not exempt from the service of preaching (Luke 2:10). The apostles have angels assisting them in completing the service of preaching and the work of the Gospel.

Divine Care and Fatherhood of God

God declares His care through His fatherhood for humans. God does not need worship or offerings from people, but He seeks their hearts, to elevate them to His glory, to enjoy His eternal love and their sonship to Him. The scholar Origen says that it is fitting for us to examine what has been written in the Old Testament very carefully in search of any prayer that calls God "Our Father who art in heaven," for so far, and despite my thorough search, I have not found a single phrase. I do not mean by that that God has not been called the Father, or that those who believed in Him were not called His children, but I have not come across in any prayer, such frankness as the Savior declared when He addressed the Father as "Father." And even if God was called "the Father," and those who believed in Him were called His children (Deuteronomy 32:6, 18, 20 and Isaiah 1:2 and Malachi 1:6), the affirmation of sonship and its steadfastness is not noticeable in the Old Testament.

10

ORIGEN AND THE DIVINE GRACE[4]

The concept of grace.

Benjamin Drewery tried to give a definition of divine grace, through the numerous works of Origen, he said: If Origen were asked to provide a definition of grace, his answer would be as follows: Grace is the power of God that is offered to humans, and this is done through the work of the Holy Spirit, to enjoy salvation for a great new life, proclaimed and spoken of in the Holy Scriptures, through Jesus Christ the incarnate Word. According to Origen, grace means the free gift of God and His blessings, generosity, and compassion.

Grace and Reward

In Origen's commentary on the words of the Apostle Paul, "Now to the one who works, his wage is not credited as a favor, but as what is due" (Romans 4:4), Origen says: There is nothing among God's gifts

---

4 Fr. Tadros Malaty: Origen, page 400 etc.

to humanity that is a repayment of a debt to God, but all is by grace. Paul was right in distinguishing between the reward related to sin and the gift of grace, as it pertains to God. God's gifts are by grace, they are the work of God's absolute mercy and not like the "wage" deserved as a reward.

Grace and Works

God does not need our good works, which are actually a sign of our response to His love, and our acceptance of His divine grace freely in our lives. God asks us for things, not because He needs them, but in order to give us good things in return out of His generosity. For to him who has, more will be given, and he will have an abundance (Luke 19:12-25), he gives the ten talents adding to them the ten that were with the one who did not work. These works are practical offerings of gratitude, and it is our duty to offer them to God. What we offer is from God's gifts to us. The Lord says, everything that the human race possesses is received from me. Lest anyone think that by his offerings, he is benefiting God. What can a person offer to God? Nothing except to give Him from the gifts He has given to him. This was evident in the case of the thief who was crucified on the right hand of our Lord Jesus, and his sins were forgiven because of his faith.

"O Lord, my heart is not proud..." These are the words of the righteous man, who was granted great and wonderful gifts and blessings, yet did not become arrogant because of them, but remained humble.

Grace and the Works of the Holy Trinity

The works of the Holy Trinity are indeed abundant gifts without payment:

First: The grace of the Father:

1. He created us through the Logos.
2. He bestowed free will upon all rational creatures as a divine gift.
3. His fatherhood to us, revealed by his only son.
4. His continuous divine care for all his creatures.
5. His satisfaction of our needs with his supreme love and gifts.
6. His unlimited love, demonstrated by the salvific work of his son, and his Holy Spirit.

Secondly: The grace of the Son:

1. A personal relationship with the only begotten Son, his title implying his grace.
2. His incarnation, crucifixion, and resurrection as the grace of salvation.
3. In him we become children of God. Through baptism, he grants us adoption to the Father as a divine grace.
4. He is our teacher and leader in the law of the Lord in our spiritual battles, as he grants us victory over evil forces.

Thirdly: The grace of the Holy Spirit:

1. He inspires us with truth, and grants us wisdom and knowledge.
2. *He gu*ides us in prayer with hearts ablaze with divine love.
3. He bestows upon us holiness and perfection.

The divine grace in the lives of believers

Grace is the enjoyment of God, the Holy Trinity, dwelling in believers and working in them. What concerned Origen was the test of unity with God, the giver of grace who became a gift for humanity to possess and be raised to his heavens. Origen's Gospel understanding sometimes led to the use of the name of Christ instead of his gifts.

Grace as a proclamation of the divine nature.

The eschatological stance (belief in the afterlife) did not lead believers to think about a debate regarding the concept of grace, but rather they immersed themselves in experiencing it and enjoying divine love. The Word of God became human for us so that we can accept Him in His greatness, He is the Christ and He is all virtues, He comes to us and speaks with us, so the kingdom of God becomes within us by being His disciples. The Savior called us: "I am the door. If anyone enters by Me, he will be saved, and will go in and out and find pasture" (John 10:9). And since the Father is not separate from the Son, He is with those who accept the Son, enjoying absolution from their sins. This is a confirmation of what the Logos stated: "Those who are well have no need of a physician, but those who are sick" (Matthew 9:12). "By the appearing of our Savior Jesus Christ" (2 Timothy 1:10), who reveals His appearance to all the perfect, and enlightens the mind with true knowledge of things. God did not send the Logos only as a physician for sinners, but also as a teacher of divine mysteries, for those who are pure. When our souls' eyes were opened by the Logos, we discern the difference between light and darkness, and we prefer to stand in the light, not in darkness. If Celsus asks us: How do we know God, and how do we find salvation in Him, we answer him that the Word of God is able to declare the Father, and make Him known to those who had not seen Him before the incarnation of the Logos. The Logos is able to save the soul of man. He became flesh so that those who could not see Him could accept Him, and thus they say: "Though we have known

Christ according to the flesh, yet now we know Him thus no longer" (2 Corinthians 5:16). "We believe" in God who revealed Himself, who manifested with His great power, and spread the principles of holiness among humans in the world. Christ alone "sees the Father" (John 6:46). Even though it is said that "the pure in heart see God" (Matthew 5:8), this is undoubtedly spiritual and through Christ. Therefore, the Savior was keen on using the correct word when He said: "No one knows the Father except the Son," and did not say "sees." For those who are concerned with seeing God, He gives them the "Spirit of knowledge" and the "Spirit of wisdom" so they can see Him through the Spirit Himself (Isaiah 11:2). That is why He said: "He who has seen Me has seen the Father" (John 14:9). It would be foolish of us to assume that those who spoke about the physical body of Jesus also saw the Father, otherwise the scribes, Pharisees, Pilate, and all the crowd who cried out "Crucify Him... Crucify Him" would have done so, as many witnessed Him, but no one "saw" Him, except those who believed that the Logos is the Son of God, and in Him the Father is also seen.

Grace and our perfection in Christ.

Divine grace gives us perfection in every virtue. If we wish to take this most perfect virtue and enjoy it within ourselves, we must first follow every means in order to achieve it with diligence that is considered perfection by human standards. If we do this, we will be careful to clear our minds that all of this is nothing without God's grace. "Let us humble ourselves under the mighty hand of God" (1 Peter 5:6), and we pray that the perfection of all goodness in us will be a gift from God, and that it will make us perfect and acceptable to God as His children.

The grace of sanctification

Rowan Greer says that Origen, in describing the greater aspect of life, borrows some excerpts from Plato. The goal of Christian life is to become holy, so we say: There is a type of food that surpasses daily bread for our existence, for which we must pray until we become worthy of it. This is provided to us by the Logos, which was from the beginning with the Father, so we become holy. Here, Origen draws on the early Christian tradition, and in particular on Clement of Alexandria's use of a passage from Plato's work theaetetus, which defines human destiny as "as closely as possible the resemblance to God." Plato also understands this destiny as a launching of the soul towards God. In the phaedrus, the soul gains wings for its return to heaven. Origen alludes to this idea, in his talk about the return of the soul like an eagle towards God. In his talk about the blessedness of the martyrs, he says that by severing their close ties, they made wings for themselves like eagles, with which they could fly to where their God was.

In his work De Principiis, Origen explained the meaning of sanctification by saying, Its aim is to hopefully become participants in the divine nature, by imitating him. It was said: "Whoever says that he abides in Him must also walk as he walked" (1 John 2:6). Jauncey says that grace - according to Origen - is not just enlightenment (the grace of baptism), but it is also participation in the perfection of Christ, in true union with divine power. Origen says: "Through the constant work of the Father, the Son, and the Holy Spirit toward us, over successive stages of progress, we become able to see the holy life and the blessedness of the saints.

Origen says, "The Spirit (Holy Spirit) is the source of our renewal, for without the Spirit, no one can participate with the Father and the Son. The love poured out by the Holy Spirit in our hearts makes us partners in the divine nature."

Quotes from Origen's writings about the role of grace in renewing our nature.

The branch cannot bear fruit unless it is firmly established in the vine, so it is the right of the disciples of the Logos, who are the rational *branches of His vine, not to produce the fruits of virtues if they are not firmly established in the true vine, the Christ of God.*

The Son of Man came indeed, but not in His glory. It was necessary for Him to come in this way, to bear our sins and suffer for us. It was not fitting for Christ in His glory to bear our sins and suffer for us. But He will come in His glory after preparing His disciples in this appearance "which has no form or beauty," by becoming like them so that they may also become like Him, "conformed to His image" (Romans 8:29). In His first coming, He was "in the likeness of human flesh" (Philippians 3:21), "emptying Himself, taking the form of a servant," so that He may restore humanity to the image of God and make them in His likeness.

By knowing that the Lord Christ came, we realize that through Him many believers are able to be like Him, loving righteousness and hating sin, so God anointed them with the oil of gladness (Psalm 45:7). He loves righteousness and hates injustice more than His companions, He received the first fruits of this oil, indeed the fullness of the oil, but His companions, each according to their abilities, shared in His anointing. Therefore, Christ is the head of the Church, meaning that Christ and the Church are one body, "the anointing flowing down from the head to the beard" of Aaron...

The Son, in His mercy, sanctified others, transforming them into gods, in the image of the first prototype, the Logos, who is the original model for many images.

The grace of our sonship to the Father

None of the writers of the Old Testament addressed God saying, "Father." This may have been because they did not know the Father. They prayed to Him as a god and master, awaiting the one who would pour out the spirit of adoption, whether on them or on those who believe in God through Him after His appearance. So if Christ did not appear to them, and they did not attain the fullness of sonship in the spirit, they did not have the boldness to speak or write about God as a Father openly.

Satan was our father before God became our Father. Everyone who commits sin is born of Satan, and we are considered born of him as long as we commit sin. This constant birth from Satan is characterized by misery as much as the birth from God is characterized by blessing. The righteous person is born on every occasion when he performs a good deed, as Christ shines in glory... In my belief, no one is entitled to address God as "Father" unless he is filled with the "spirit of adoption" (Romans 8:15)... "Love your enemies so that you may be sons of your Father who is in heaven." Everyone who practices righteousness (1 John 2:29) is born of God (1 John 3:9). Since he cannot sin thereafter, he is entitled to say "Father." Man is born of God, through the living Word of God, as it is written "But to all who did receive him, who believed in his name, he gave the right to become children of God, who were born, not of blood nor of the will of the flesh nor of the will of man, but of God" (John 1:12).

Grace and Heavenly Life

Divine grace makes our hearts close to the heavens, giving us the longing to attain the heavenly kingdom, not only in the world to come, but also here on earth, where Christ dwells in us. Origen says: [As long as Christ Jesus, the divine Logos, who was with God from the beginning, does not dwell in the soul, the kingdom of heaven is not there. And when a person is ready to receive the Logos, the kingdom of heaven is within reach of his right hand.]

Grace and Participation in the Crucifixion of Christ

Divine grace enables us to participate in the crucifixion, death, and resurrection of Christ.

The Holy Gospel as Divine Grace

The Holy Spirit reveals the truth to us, and gives us the Holy Scriptures as divine grace. As we read and listen to the Scriptures and understand its words, we have the opportunity to be in the presence of God. The divine Scriptures say that the written word, even if it is most convincing in itself, is not sufficient to reach the human soul unless God gives power to the speaker; this power is obtained by those who teach with action. Nothing good comes apart from God, especially in relation to understanding the Holy Scriptures. Let us implore God to grant us the word with breadth and richness in contemplating Christ Jesus. Through this, we can hear the sacred words. If sometimes we fail to understand some of what is said, that should not diminish our obedience, but it is worthy for us to be patient until God inspires us with answers to our questions, either through direct enlightenment or through the mediation of others.

Divine Grace and Praise to God

The divine grace changes our inner selves so that we can enjoy the kingdom of the joyful Lord and we can sing praises to the glory of God. The elevation of man in every virtue and in the life of wisdom is to glorify the one who dwells within himself.

Grace and satisfaction: We can only satisfy ourselves through the work of divine grace, through which we accept God himself to dwell in our inner selves, and we receive grace from God and are filled with His gifts.

God is the God of the living who recognize the grace He has bestowed upon them, when He declared that He is their God and said, "This is my covenant with you and your descendants" (Exodus 3:15). So Abraham, Isaac, and Jacob lived in awareness of God and His grace.

Grace without payment

Grace is a gift from God, given to those who are not able to earn it on their own. Saint Paul says, "being justified freely by His grace" (Romans 3:24). It is not a divine gift to humanity that is a payment for a debt, but all are gifts, as human nature cannot attain virtue without help from above. Origen affirms that divine grace, which is without payment, always works in the life of the believer, giving him the good will and the ability to live a new life in Christ. Believers cannot perform righteousness without divine grace. At the same time, God, who gives man free will as the greatest gift, does not work in him against his will, but gives him the right to accept or reject His grace. This grace is not something static or passive, but dynamic, always effective. Therefore, the believer who accepts it enjoys constant growth so as not to lose it. The apostle says, "Do not quench the Spirit" (1 Thessalonians 5:19). With His wisdom, God offers great grace to those who show with all their strength that they love Him.

Sometimes the holy fire may go out, even in the saints. We hear the apostle Paul warning those who are deemed worthy of the gifts of the Spirit and grace, saying, "Do not quench the Spirit" (1 Thessalonians 5:19).

The Bible says about Jacob, "Jacob's spirit revived" (Genesis 45:27), as if his soul was renewed when he was told that Joseph was still alive. And upon hearing that Joseph had become "ruler over all the land of Egypt." The fact that his son had subdued Egypt under his rule. Whoever has subdued some of the vices of his body, and continued to surrender to others and submit to them, cannot be said to be "ruler over all the land of Egypt," but it can be said that he is a ruler over a city or two of it. As for Joseph, who had freed himself from all bodily desires, his spirit was ignited.

The measure of grace

Origen affirms that God assists humans by granting them His grace, which is without merit. He desires to bestow it upon them limitlessly, but gives it according to the following criteria:

1. *God's grace exceeds our needs, but we only receive what we require.*

2. *It is according to the will of God (Romans 12:6, 1 Corinthians 12:7, 11).*

3. *Our faith is expressed through actions and virtues. Grace is given "by faith" (Romans 4:16), and its purpose is to collaborate in adorning faith with deeds.*

11

ORIGEN AND GOD THE FATHER

Origen states that the birth of the Son is eternal and continuous, as the Father begets the Son in every moment, if the expression is correct, just as light gives its rays or splendor continuously. The birth of the Son of God is eternal and continuous, and Origen says that eternity is a unique moment that cannot be expressed in any human language. The Son is born from the Father like the radiance from light, or the emanation of will or word from the mind. As Origen says, this birth, among its titles, is called wisdom in the Book of Wisdom of Solomon (7:25-26), and it is the splendor of the glory of the Father, a very pure emanation of the Almighty's glory. It is mentioned in the interpretations and contemplations of the early fathers of the Book of Wisdom, by the author: [The Lord Christ is called the "Wisdom of God," the splendor of the Father's glory, for if God is light, there cannot be light without splendor, nor splendor without light. There is no time that separates light from splendor. Therefore, if the wisdom of God is one with the Father in essence, and calls Himself: "I am the light of the world," He is also called "the splendor of light." He shines upon souls, so they may come into contact with the light and recognize it. "The only Son, who is in the bosom of the Father, has made Him known" (John 1:18). He is the Word of the Father, speaking to us not through disconnected words, but through the radiance of wisdom upon us.]

Origen's logic against Sabellius led to insisting that the Logos was distinct from the Father, and eternal (i.e. timeless and everlasting), so no one could dare to speak of a beginning for the Son and that at some point he did not exist. This eternal birth, the Son has no beginning, contrary to what Arianism claimed. The eternity of this birth is certainly clear, because it is unreasonable to think that the Father was without his wisdom, mind, and word that refers to the Son. Or that the Father had a beginning at a certain time, as if he did not exist from eternity, so the change in the Lord cannot be believed. This idea is found twice in Origen's book "Principles" and once in Paul the Apostle's letter to the Romans. We find this famous passage that he used against the Arians: Is it possible to believe that the Father is the eternal light, and that his glory was not with him? And if so, there was never a time when the Son was not the Son.

Between the fatherhood of God to the only begotten Son and the sonship of the children by adoption.

The relationship between the Father and the Son differs from the relationship between the Lord and the creature (i.e. humans). The Apostle Paul says: "For all who are led by the Spirit of God are sons of God. For you did not receive the spirit of slavery to fall back into fear, but you have received the Spirit of adoption as sons, by whom we cry, 'Abba! Father!'" (Romans 8:14-15).

When Origen speaks of the hypostasis (person) of the Father, he says that the Father is the source of existence, not taking his existence from another. Without any compromise on the equality of the hypostases (persons) in the Trinity, Origen can teach that the Father is the origin of all existence and the source of all goodness.

The goodness and justice of the Father.

The second part of Origen's work "First Principles" was directed against the Gnostics, especially the Marcionites. Origen does not accept the separation between the Creator, the Lord of the Old Covenant, and the Father in the New Covenant, but always proclaims that the Creator Lord is the Father, and the holy Paul does the same. While some heretics attribute justice to the Creator and love to the Father, Origen affirms that there is no justice without love and goodness, just as there is no goodness without justice. So when the Father punishes, he does so out of righteousness. And the Lord is called righteous in the Old Covenant as he is in the New Covenant.

The Father is not the creator of evil.

The Father is the origin and creator of everything, even matter, but he is not the creator of sin and evil. Sins and evils are not positive facts, but negative, and sin is "nothing."

Christ reveals the Father in the Old Covenant and in the New Covenant.

God the Father is known through His creatures. Usually, we do not see the nature of light itself with our eyes, but when we see its rays either through windows or small openings where light enters, we can understand how light is emitted. Similarly, the works of divine care emit as a kind of rays. So, if we understand that we cannot know the Lord as He is, then we know Him through the beauty of His works and creatures.

1. **The divine Word reveals the Father even in the Old Testament: The Word inspired people before His incarnation, and gave believers divine knowledge. And before that time, the Word of the Lord was in Moses and the prophets.**

2. **We must know the Father through the incarnation of the Word: The Father, who is not easy to understand, we perceive through the Word, who became human. And He gave His believers the gift of union with the Father in Him, thus they knew Him. And through this knowledge, the soul returns to its original righteousness.**

   Joseph C. Mclelland says that the incarnation of the Word gives us the ability to know Him. Here, Origen's Platonism differs from the classical tradition that appears in Celsus. Plato says that it is difficult to comprehend the Creator of this universe. It is unreasonable for human nature to comprehend the degree suitable for the Father. We affirm that human nature, if helped by the Lord, realizes that He is the Creator. The goal of faith is to know the Lord through His union with the Son, who alone knows Him. The Word of the Lord meets those who seek Him and accept Him when He reveals Himself, and He is able to introduce the Father to those who have not seen Him at His coming.

3. We, who have practical knowledge of the Father, can be connected to Him through our Savior, who became the High Priest and the Giver. Christ is the High Priest who, with His blood, made you connected to the Father. We have peace with the Lord (Romans 1:5) through the Lord Jesus who connected us to Him through His blood. Christ came to crush the enemies and grant peace, and connect us to the Father when we are separated from Him because of our sins. And we can draw near to Him through Jesus Christ, especially when we realize that He is the righteousness, truth, wisdom, resurrection, and true light, because we cannot draw near to the Lord or to the truth without peace and Christ.

   The characteristics of Christ enable us to know the Father. The Logos gives us the intellect through which we know the Father.

He is the light of the world, illuminating our inner vision in the Father. He is the truth that connects us to Him, so that we may attain divine knowledge. Therefore, our Savior is the image of the unseen Father. He is the truth and the image through which we know the Father, whom no one knows, and whom the Son is pleased to reveal to us. All who believe are certain that "grace and truth come through Jesus Christ" (John 1:17). And those who recognize Christ as the truth agree with His statement: "I am the truth" (John 14:6), receiving the knowledge that enables a person to live a righteous life, derived from the words of Christ spoken when He became incarnate.

The Father gives us to His beloved Son.

The Father gives us to the Son, our teacher and healer, to free us from ignorance and illness, that is, from sin, and to protect us to be under the divine royal rule.

- ❖ In general, before the incarnation of the only begotten Son, many men of the Old Covenant were unable to know the Lord as their Father. Perhaps because they did not know the Father, they offered their prayers to Him as the Lord and God, expecting to receive the spirit of sonship, like those who believed in the Lord through Him after His appearance.

12

ORIGEN AND JESUS CHRIST[1]

Some brothers wonder about Origen's position on the Subordination theory, and I have republished the book "Jesus Christ according to Origen," as it provides a good answer to this question. Despite the abundance of excerpts from the writings of Origen about our loving Savior in this book, they are considered very few examples of what he wrote about our Savior. In this simple work, we engage with Origen's view of the Lord Christ and his experiences in union with him. These excerpts highlighted the following:

1. Our Christ is eternal, there was never a time when he did not exist, because the Father was never without the Son from eternity, and he was never separated from the Son at any moment, because he is the wisdom of God and the power of God (1 Cor 1:24).

2. Our Christ, in his divinity, is not limited to a specific place, he fills the heavens and the earth.

3. His incarnation and descent to our earth was a voluntary act,

---

[1] From: Our Christ, the Lover of Mankind, Second Revised Edition, 2020.

as it was said: "He loved me and gave himself for me" (Gal 2:20). His descent did not make his hypostasis less than that of the Father, but it was the joy of the Father and the Holy Spirit to practically declare the divine love of the Son for humanity through his sufferings, crucifixion, resurrection, and ascension to heaven. And as the Son himself said: "For God so loved the world that he gave his one and only Son, that whoever believes in him shall not perish but have eternal life" (John 3:16). A descent for his divine plan and care for humanity, without any change in essence, as he is one with the Father and the Holy Spirit in the same divine essence.

4. Origen affirmed that our Christ became a true human, honoring humanity in the eyes of the heavenly beings, sanctifying our bodies, senses, emotions, along with our souls and minds.

5. By his incarnation, he united us to himself to renew and develop our nature and grant us the companionship of eternal inheritance.

6. On the cross, he proclaimed to us the divine love, defeated Satan and all his forces, conquered death, and made believers his mystical body, as he became the head of the holy Church.

Salvation does not stop at the forgiveness of our sins, but it presents our reconciliation with the Holy Trinity. We enjoy the Lord Jesus as the heavenly priest, physician, teacher, heavenly bread that satisfies souls, the true light, the wisdom of God, the power of God, the divine truth, and the way that leads us to the embrace of the Father. He is the king who dwells within us to establish his kingdom inside us and make us kings. He opens our hearts with love so that we desire to serve every person. He is the hidden treasure, the true joy, the bridegroom of our souls, making us part of the household of God and satisfying all our needs.

The excerpts in your hands, beloved, are not for dry argumentative dialogue, but for us to acquire them with joy and love, so that we may reclaim the image of God within us. Our lives, worship, and even our hidden thoughts become a living testimony to divine love, attracting many to desire to cling to our loving Christ. With God's will, I hope to continue this work by publishing a book on "Responding to the heresy of the gradation between the divine hypostases" adopted by the heretic Arius.

What motivates writing about the one God in His divinity and about each hypostasis of the three hypostases?

Origen's concern for dialogue with heretics to testify to the divine truth so that believers do not stumble, to refute heretics of their error, and to invite them to enjoy practical communion with God.

Revealing the role of doctrine in the life of the Church, the people, and the priests, without being preoccupied with dry rational debates at the expense of continuous growth and spiritual edification, while not neglecting the gift of reason bestowed by God upon humans along with the continuous need for sanctification.

Constant sense of divine presence.

Practical enjoyment of the glorified life, the joy of the spirit, tasting the pledge of heaven while we are still in the flesh amidst the troubles of life in the world and the never-ending trials of Satan. Enjoying the blessing of our Lord and Savior Jesus Christ.

Jesus Christ and His role in the lives of believers.[2]

The scholar Origen, in his writings and teachings, focused on the Lord Jesus, as his heart was aflame with love for Him, finding in Him satisfaction for all his needs. He urges us to accept Him as the truth,

---

[2] Chapter Nine from the book Origen by the author, 1995, with adaptation.

the heavenly teacher, the physician, the remedy, the only righteousness that heals our souls from corruption, the kingdom, the heavenly bread, the hidden treasure, the divine way, the door, the rock, the resurrection, the beginning, and the end.

Origen believed that the human soul had fallen from its heavenly rank, and after being free, it became unable to regain its origin without the Lord Christ.

With his unlimited love, the Savior extends his hands to humanity to bestow upon it eternal glory, but not by force.

As we made ourselves slaves to Satan by practicing sin, the Lord Christ gave his blood out of love as the price for our freedom.

Our Christ, the Savior of the world, is the high priest and the sacrifice, offering his life as a sacrifice for us.

Jesus Christ is the heavenly bridegroom, working for his spiritual union with our souls as his bride.

Origen sees the Old Testament as a whole speaking of him as the joyful Messiah.

Christ, the lover of humanity

Origen believed that our Lord Jesus Christ is the Savior of humanity. The Lord Christ gave himself for them, loving humans even when they were sinners and enemies, seeking to enter into a personal relationship with the human soul.[3]

❖ *The Apostle Paul expressed what was written about Adam and Eve: "This is a great mystery, but I speak concerning Christ and the church" (Ephesians 5:32). He loved her and gave himself*

---

3 Some scribes, in order to distort his image, added that he believed in the renewal of all creation, including the devil and his evil angels.

for her. While she was disobedient, it was said: "While we were still sinners, Christ died for us" (Romans 5:8).[4]

- *It was said of "Jesus" that he was "raised in glory," and in that I see the grace of God for me.*[5]

The Divinity of the Lord Christ

The eternal Son of God: Origen believes that the personality of the divine Word is not limited to a mission[6]**. The Son is Hypostasis, that is, the living Wisdom. He is God essentially and truly. Therefore, necessarily, he is a partner with the Father in his eternity and equal to him. The birth of the Son is eternal and continuous. The Father begets the Son at every moment, as he continuously gives his light. Origen's understanding of his eternity**[7] **and continuity cannot be expressed in human language.**[8]

- There was no time when (the Son) did not exist. When God, whom John called the Light, is not just about the radiance of his glory, so that man dares to specify a beginning to the existence of the Son, let man who dares to say that there was a time when the Son did not exist realize that his statement is equivalent to claiming that at some point there was no wisdom, no Word for God, and no life.[9]

- None of those testimonies clearly highlight the glorious birth of the Savior. But when the words are directed to him: "You are my son, today I have begotten you" (Psalm 7:2; Mark 11:1; Hebrews 5:1) the one addressing him is God (the Father) who

---

4 *Comm. on the Songs of Songs, book 2:3 (ACW).*
5 *Contra Celsus 3:31.*
6 *R. Cadiou: Origen, Herder Book Co., 1944, p. 290.*
7 *In Jer. hom. 9:4.*
8 *Henri Crouzel: Origen, San Francisco 1989, p. 187.*
9 *De Principiis 4:28; Charles Bigg: The Christian Platonists of Alexandria, p. 207-208.*

considers all time in relation to him as today. He has no evening or morning, but rather an extended time in harmony with a life that has no beginning. For him, today is the day on which his son was born, and there is no existence of the beginning of his birth.[10]

- ❖ We acknowledge that God is the Father of his only begotten son, who truly was born from him, and derives his being through him. But without a beginning, not only of the kind that is distinguished by a chronological date, but even of another kind that the mind alone cannot contemplate or comprehend through abstract or logical thought.

John (the Evangelist) uses lofty and wonderful language in the opening of his gospel where he defines the Word as God. "In the beginning was the Word, and the Word was with God" (John 1:1-2). Whoever defines the beginning of the Word of God or the wisdom of God, warns against committing evil towards the Father who is not born of himself. This is when it is denied that he has always been a Father. And that he begets the Word and has wisdom, in previous times and seasons or however they are called.

The beginning of eternity and the end of eternity, like splendor emanating from light. He does not become a son through an external means through the spirit of adoption, but he is a son by nature. And now, as we have said before, the wisdom of God does not return in its existence except to him, who is also the one who was born of it. And since he himself is the only begotten son by nature, he is this wisdom, on this basis he is also called "the only begotten son."[11]

---

10 *Comm. on John 1:32 (ANF)*.
11 *De Principiis 1:2:2-5 (Cf. Butterworth)*.

The eternal wisdom of God

❖ Since the wisdom of God, who is his only begotten son, is by all measures unchangeable or replaceable, and since all the good qualities in him are essential, and cannot be changed or replaced, his glory on this basis is described as purity and truth... And now the wisdom of God is that light, not only in being light, but in being an eternal light. His wisdom is therefore an infinite and eternal splendor. If you fully grasp this point, it is a clear indication that the existence of the son emanates from the Father alone; but not in time, and not from any other beginning except God himself as we have said.[12]

❖ Christ is the comprehensive wisdom. As for the understanding of wisdom in any wise person, it is actually a partnership in Christ.[13]

His theology is unlimited in place.

Origen affirms in his work De Principiis the theology of the Lord Christ, who is unlimited in place, and therefore is not of progression, and is not of greater hypostasis and lesser hypostasis.

❖ Some may wonder that through those considered partners (Heb 14:3) in the word of God or in His wisdom or truth or life, it seems as if the word itself and wisdom are limited in a specific place. To answer this question, it must be emphasized that Christ, being the Logos and Wisdom and more, was present in Paul who said: "Since you seek a proof of Christ speaking in me" (2 Cor 3:13). He also says: "I live, yet not I, but Christ lives in me" (Gal 2:20). Therefore, since he was present in Paul, who doubts that he was also present in Peter and in John and in every

---

12 *De Principiis 1:2:11 (Cf. Butterworth)*.
13 *Comm. on John 1:34*.

saint among the saints. Indeed, he was not only present on earth, but also in those in heaven. It is ridiculous to say that Christ was in Paul and in Peter, and was not in both the chief angels Michael and Gabriel. From this, it is clear that the theology of the Son of God was not limited in place, as he was not in one without the other, but rather, he was not limited in place due to the glory of his non-physical nature, so we understand that he is not absent from any place... and his existence is not similar in all beings. He is more complete and clearer, or in other words, more explicit in the heads of the angels than in the holy humans, and the evidence for that is when the saints reach the highest ranks, it is said that they have become "like angels or equal to angels," as mentioned in the Gospel (Matt 30:22; Luke 36:20). Therefore, Christ is present in various people, according to their merits.

David refers to the mystery of the complete Trinity in creating everything by saying: "By the word of the Lord the heavens were made, and all the host of them by the breath of His mouth" (Psalm 33:6). And John the Baptist refers to something similar in his address to the crowds while Christ was absent from them in the flesh, saying: "There stands One among you whom you do not know. It is He who, coming after me, is preferred before me, whose sandal strap I am not worthy to loose" (John 1:26-27). John could not have said that the Lord Christ was standing among those who were not present with him in the flesh. He was absent in terms of his physical presence. From this, it is evident that the Son of God is fully present in the flesh, as he is fully present everywhere.

The Divine Incarnation and the Divinity of the Lord Christ

Origen affirmed this truth, that the Lord Christ became human, and yet he is God.

❖ *Jesus Christ, who came to earth, was born of the Father before all creation. And after becoming a worker for the Father in establishing all things, "through him all things were made" (John 1:3) He emptied Himself and became human despite being God. That is, "being in very nature God, did not consider equality with God something to be used to his own advantage" (Philippians 2:6).*

He took on a body like ours, only differing in that He was born of a virgin and by the Holy Spirit.

This Jesus Christ was truly born and suffered, not in appearance. He died in reality our complete death. And also rose in reality from death, and ascended to heaven after His resurrection.[14]

❖ Also, listen to what Paul says: "You are God's field, God's building" (1 Corinthians 3:9). So what is that sacred building not made by human hands, but prepared by God's hand? Let us heed what wisdom says: "Wisdom has built her house" (Proverbs 9:1). I believe that this can be understood more accurately in the divine incarnation, which did not happen through human planting. That is, the structure of the body was not built by the Virgin through human work. Rather, as Daniel prophesied: "a stone was cut out, but not by human hands, and it struck the statue on its feet of iron and clay and smashed them" (Daniel 2:34-35). This is the sacred building of the body that was (cut out) from the mountain of human nature and from the material of the flesh (not by human hands), that is, without human work.[15]

Under the title "God Unchanging but Full of Life," Joseph C. McLelland addresses Origen's view on the incarnation of the Logos, that is, the Word, saying: [For Origen, he dealt with this issue using expressions

---

14 *De Principiis 1:1:4 (Cf. Butterworth).*
15 *In Exodus hom.6:12 (Cf. Ronad E Heine- Frs. of the Church, vol. 71.)*

that gained the Platonic doctrine... He faced extreme difficulty in all of this. Where he opposed (the Stoics, Epicureans, and even Aristotle) who filled the world with a doctrine calling for the abolition of divine care or its limitation, or advancing a principle of a corruptible material first, while they considered the Jewish and Christian doctrine preserving the divine nature unchangeable or replaceable, and unworthy of respect for contradicting those who hold erroneous views about God...][16]

The Word came into the world through divine incarnation.[17] The Gospel truth is undoubtedly embodied in the realization of its acceptance in a human reality with an elevation to a divine reality that transcends it. The divine descent into the world through the incarnation was a decisive matter for all Origen's theologians, as Celsus objected, "If we affirm that God will descend to humans, does this imply - in his opinion - that He will leave His throne?"[18] Origen responds to this objection: "Celsus does not comprehend the power of God, who fills all things while everything retains its essence. So, if it is said that God descended or came to us, it does not mean that He moved from one place to another, or that He left His throne. The matter does not involve change or abandonment."[19] "Even if we were to assume that He left one place and filled another, we do not say that in the sense of 'place.' So, in what sense do we mean it then? In the sense of existence. For change must be understood as happening within us. For anyone who personally receives the coming of the Word of God in their spirit changes from wicked to righteous, from lack of commitment to self-control, and from irrationality to piety. And as one scholar concludes about Origen: "The earthly life of Christ was a divine secret narrative aimed at enlightening humanity."[20]

---

16 *Contra Celsus 1:21; Joseph c. McLelland: God The Anonymous, Massachusetts, 1976,* p. 106-107.
17 *Joseph c. McLelland: God The Anonymous, Massachusetts, p. 113.*
18 *Contra Celsus 4:5.*
19 *Cf. Contra Celsus 6:60.*
20 *Joseph c. McLelland: God The Anonymous, p. 117.*

Origen takes us back to his previous answer, then adds: "While remaining unchanged in essence, he descends for his divine providence and care for the human race." This doctrine distinguishes itself from that embraced by the Stoics and the Epicureans, who did not have a clear understanding of "the true concept of the nature of God, in that it is incorruptible and indivisible, as well as simple." Christ also was in the image of God,[21] but he emptied himself so that he could be accepted by humans. "Yet he did not undergo any change from good to evil." When the Word assumed human flesh and human soul, the Word remained in essence without experiencing what the body or soul undergo. His descent was to the lowest level, for those unable to accept divine providence. "He became flesh and was described in bodily terms, so that by the Word, those who accept him in this form gradually ascend, until he is exalted, if it is permissible to express his absolute state."[22] The situation varies according to the types of recipients, whether they are beginners, advanced, have achieved tangible progress, or have almost reached virtue or actually reached it."[23] Those at the lowest level were unable to face the more truthful image that Jesus showed to the few on the mountain. The former only saw the mortal nature. Origen uses Isaiah's statement "he had no form or majesty" (53:2), while the disciples perceived the image of the eternal Logos.[24]

Origen did not imply that the human form was merely an appearance; he is "not deceitful or lying." Despite not stating that the incarnate form shares in an absolute attribute (meaning the body did not change into the divine nature), at the same time he does not claim the opposite, in a Gnostic way, descending with the incarnation to appearance... that is, a type of manifestation. He affirmed the reality of the incarnation, that it is a teaching that works within us. The divine Logos took on humanity

---

21 *Contra Celsus 4:15.*
22 *Joseph c. McLelland: God The Anonymous, p. 119.*
23 *Joseph c. McLelland: God The Anonymous, p. 119.*
24 *Contra Celsus 4:16.*

for our actual fallen state, "thus it becomes possible for us to accept him initially."[25][26]

Jesus Christ was a real human.

Origen does not deny the reality of the body of the Lord Jesus, and he truly needed sustenance.[27] His life, pains, and sufferings were not in any way fake, but Origen believes that the body of Jesus was real.[28]

- ❖ The body of Satan, by its nature, is composed of a subtle substance like air, so most people (the heretics) consider it non-physical. As for the Savior, his body was tangible and able to be interacted with...[29]

Origen faced the deep "composite nature" of Christ.[30] With his acknowledgment that the Logos took on a body no different from human flesh, thus "taking with the body what accompanies it of pains and sorrows."[31] However, he knows that the pains of Christ and his death fall at the forefront of divine love and salvation.[32] Here he speaks of the "benefit" of Christ's death, and proves it, starting from the reality of his pains to the reality of his resurrection.[33]

Origen is considered to have enriched Greek Christian theology with terms such as physis, hypostasis, ousia, homousios, and theonthropos. He was the first to use the title of the God-Man (theonthropos) to affirm the humanity of Jesus in his confrontation with the Gnostics. He also affirmed the unity of the nature of the Lord Christ in saying

---

25 *Contra Celsus 4:18.*
26 *Comm. on John 1:20; Joseph c. McLelland: God The Anonymous.*
27 *In Gal., Frag., Tollinton: Selections from the Commentaries and Homilies of Origen, SPCK 1929, p 41ff; Joseph c. McLelland: God The Anonymous, p. 121.*
28 *Bigg: The Christian Platonists of Alexandria, p. 234.*
29 *De Principiis 1:2:2-5 (Cf. Butterworth).*
30 *Contra Celsus 1:66.*
31 *Contra Celsus 2:23.*
32 *Contra Celsus 1:54f., 61.*
33 *Contra Celsus 2:16.*

that the Lord Christ, despite being named with a title that includes the meaning of his divinity, his human attributes can predict him, and vice versa, saying:[34]

- ❖ The Son of God, through whom all things were created, was called Jesus Christ, also called the Son of Man. It was also said, "The Son of God died."

- ❖ The Son of Man, who was announced to come with the angels of the saints in the glory of God the Father, was called.

- ❖ The divine nature was not mentioned throughout the entire Bible in human language only, but the human nature was honored with designations specific to divine dignity.[35]

- ❖ After the incarnation, the soul of Jesus became one with the Word of God.[36]

His body took shape

- ❖ The Word appears in different forms according to the capacity of each individual. For some, he was "without form or beauty," and for others, he was flourishing with beauty. And for those who were still in the stage of ascent through glorious works, leading them to the high mountain of wisdom, he was seen in a simpler form, known for bodily concepts. As for the perfect ones, he was perceived in his divinity, and their knowledge qualified them to see him in the form of God.[37]

---

34   *In Ez. hom. 3:3.*
35   *De Princ. 2,6,3 ANF.*
36   *Contra Celsus 2:9.*
37   *Frag. Hom. Luke 15 (On Transfiguration).*

Christ has a human soul

Charles Bigg says: Origen was the first to speak extensively about the human soul of Jesus. He also said that Origen believes that all human souls existed before the body. And we do not know if these texts were put forth by his opponents to affirm that he was a heretic or whether he fell into this error influenced by some philosophers.

The body of Jesus was pure from all the impurities of birth, and from all types of filth, and it was a real body. In his book De Principiis, Origen affirmed that the Lord Christ had a human soul.[38]

❖ When the Son of God wanted to appear to people and live among them for the salvation of the human race, He did not only take on a human body, but also took on a human soul that resembles our souls in its nature, but does not resemble Him in intention and ability, so that it can be satisfied without giving up the desires and measures of the Word and Wisdom.

The Goals of the Incarnation

Benjamin Drewery gives us a summary of Origen's opinion regarding the goals of the Incarnation, saying: The Lord Christ became like humans so that they may become like Him. He provided all that is good, teaching the way to God, warning of judgment, presenting Himself as an example of ideal life, bringing about change, reform, and purification from evils, bringing joy to His followers, sowing the seeds of the Word of God, and opening up the kingdom of God to the whole world, whether deserving or undeserving, and even to those who are unwilling (for He offers salvation, but not by force).[39]

---

[38] Bigg: *The Christian Platonists of Alexandria* p. 233.
[39] Benjamin Drewery: *Origen and the Doctrine of Grace*, London 1960, p. 113.

The First Goal of the Incarnation: Connects us to Him and guides the nations

❖ Let us consider how the Son can elevate in the flesh to possess the virtues, which are already His by virtue of His divinity. Those who are in the world, in that they belong to the Father, can also be considered to belong, in some way, to the Son, who is a partner with the Father in His purposes. All nations are given to Him as an inheritance, and His rule extends to the ends of the earth (Psalm 2). This is because man, in his avoidance of serving God, has rebelled limitlessly against God. While the Father, the Creator, provided everything for the liberation of humans by sending the Logos, His only Son, into the world, and gave Him a body, without any change in His divine nature, to grant freedom to the captives and restore sight to the blind. Therefore, the Son has obtained His kingdom, and it has been acknowledged that He is the heir of the Father. But if we can say that, based on His human nature, we must be cautious not to misunderstand the internal structure of the mystery of the Trinity.[40]

❖ When Jesus is among the crowds, He is outside His house (Matthew 1:13), because the crowds are outside the house. This reveals His love for humans.[41]

He guides the "lost sheep of Israel," and due to their lack of faith, He takes the kingdom of God away from the Jews (who are determined to reject the Savior) and gives it to other vineyard keepers.[42]

---

40   *Benjamin Drewery: Origen and the Doctrine of Grace, London 1960, p. 113.*
41   *Fr. Malaty: Luke, p. 294 (in Arabic).*
42   *Contra Celsus 4:3.*

The Second Goal: Renews our nature

The Lord became human to restore our fallen human nature and transform it from earth to heaven.

- ❖ My Lord and Savior took on a earthly body, in His desire to establish what descended to earth, so that He may carry it up from the earth to the heavens.[43]

- ❖ Nothing good happens among humans without the work of the divine Word.[44]

Saint Paul clearly explains in the Letter to the Hebrews the difference between animal sacrifice and the sacrifice of the Lord Christ. The former is repeated due to its weakness and inadequacy in renewing the depths of human nature. The latter was offered only once, but still has the power to renew our inner selves. Origen says that Jesus Christ, as both priest and sacrifice at the same time, did not offer animal blood that perishes, but He offered His blood, which gives life, resurrection, and eternity. He elevates believers from submission to the rule of death to enjoying eternity, liberating their nature so they bear His likeness.

- ❖ He appeared in His bodily form and gave Himself as a body, attracting the two bodily beings to Himself and transforming them first into the likeness of the Word, who became flesh.[45]

- ❖ *He overflowed with His love, becoming a God to others who, through Him, were transformed into gods, as a model. The Word is the Archetype model for many images.*[46]

In his commentary on the Gospel of John, Origen determines that the word "Jordan" means "their descent into the depths." The Christ, the Savior, is the "Jordan," in which we descend to be purified. In another

---

43   *Homilies on Leviticus 9:2 (Cf. Frs. of the Church).*
44   *Contra Celsus 6:78.*
45   *Contra Celsus 6:68.*
46   *Comm. on John 2:2.*

expression, the Logos descended in His incarnation and became human, so that we may descend in turn and possess Him, for our purification.[47]

- ❖ When we contemplate those immense and wonderful truths about the nature of the Son of God, we are filled with great astonishment, as He emptied Himself of His lofty place above all, and of His royal position, to become a man, and to live among humans. This is a fact witnessed by the grace that flowed from His lips, and the testimony given by the Heavenly Father about Him, as confirmed by the signs and wonders He performed. Before His physical appearance, the prophets were sent as messengers to announce His coming. After His ascension to heaven, He transformed His holy messengers, the simple and uneducated ones from the ranks of tax collectors and fishermen, into vessels filled with His divine power, so they could roam the earth, gathering believers dedicated to Him from every nation and every race. Therefore, when we see in Him aspects that reach in His humanity to a degree not much different from the prevailing weakness in mortals, and other aspects that reach in His divinity to what is only in line with the fundamental divine nature, human understanding is bewildered. Amazement strikes him in the face of this immense miracle, not knowing which way to turn, or what to do. For when he thinks of God, he sees a man before him, and when he thinks of man, he sees someone rising from death after conquering the kingdom of death.[48]

- ❖ We must understand that "the Jordan" is the word of God who became flesh and dwelt among us, Jesus is our chief cornerstone, who gives us His humanity that He took as an inheritance from the Lord, which was elevated to the divinity of the Son of God, washed, then accepted in His essence the pure and

---

47 *Comm. on John, book 6:25.*
48 *De Principiis 2:6:1 (Cf. Butterworth).*

innocent dove of the Holy Spirit, and became connected to it, as it cannot fly far from it afterwards.[49]

- ❖ "For the falling and rising of many" (Luke 34:2): The first is for those who remain in sin, they must fall and die in it, and the second requires the sinner to rise and live in righteousness. Faith in Christ bestows these gifts of grace.[50]

- ❖ If we have risen with Christ who is righteousness, and walked in the seriousness of life, and lived according to His righteousness, then Christ rose for us to be justified. Therefore, Christ justifies only those who have taken on a new life according to the example of His resurrection, and have cast off the old garments of sin that lead to death.[51]

The third goal: to grant victory over sin, over the evil world, and over the devil.

- ❖ Jesus the Son of God, my Lord, gives me the command to crush under my feet the spirit of fornication, and to trample the neck of the spirit of wrath and anger, and the spirit of greedy lust.[52]

- ❖ Before the coming of our Lord and Savior, the demons ruled over the minds and bodies of people, and settled in their souls. Then the grace of the Lord Savior appeared, and His mercy on earth, teaching us how every person should regain freedom and restore the image of God they were created on. Who can offer this, if not Jesus Christ, who with His stripes healed us, the believers in Him, when He "disarmed the rulers and author-

---

49 *Comm. on John, book 6:25.*
50 *In Luke Hom. 17 on 2:34.*
51 *Comm. on Rom. 4:7 on 4:23-25.*
52 *In Josh. Homily 12:3..*

ities" among us and openly triumphed over them on the cross? (Colossians 2:15).[53]

❖ We fell under the rule of our enemies, that is "the ruler of this age" and his allies from the forces of evil. This is why we needed redemption through the One who bought us so that we may return from the state of estrangement from Him. Therefore, our Savior shed His blood as a ransom for us. Since forgiveness of sins that follows redemption is impossible before man is liberated, we must first be liberated from the rule of the one who took us captive and kept us under his control, so that we may be freed from his reach, in order to receive forgiveness for our sins and be healed from the wounds of sin, and to perform acts of piety and other virtues.[54]

The fourth goal: It grants us victory over death.

❖ Whoever is with Christ is above the realm of the rule of death.[55]

❖ As He rose from death once, and made His disciples fully convinced of the reality of His resurrection, they revealed to everyone through their sufferings that their eyes are fixed on eternal life, and on the resurrection that was manifested to them in word and deed, enabling them to despise all the hardships of this life.[56]

---

53 *Contra Celsus 1:54f.*
54 *Comm. on Eph. 4 on 1.*
55 *Comm. on Matt. 16:8 on 20:25-28.*
56 *Contra Celsus 2:77.*

The fifth goal: It grants us true active knowledge "Gnosis".

Origen says that the Logos is our teacher who gave us the Law and the example, and granted us connection with Him,[57]

So we lose the nature of death and irrationality and become divine and wise. He is also an example of complete life and true virtue, Christians transform into His example, enabling them to partake in the divine nature.[58][59][60][61]

- ❖ Within the theology of the Word is power, not only to assist the sick and heal them, but also to proclaim the mysteries to the pure in body and mind. The Word was sent as a physician to sinners, and as a teacher to those who are already pure.[62]

- ❖ The darkness of heretical teachings dissipates through the light of the Word. The Word opens the eyes of our souls, so we can discern between light and darkness, and choose in every situation to remain in the light.[63]

The sixth goal: We accept Him as the head of our kind.

- ❖ As Adam is the first example for us and the head of our race by nature of birth, we consider him as one body, and we record Christ, the second Adam, as our head through divine renewal,

---

[57] Kelly, p. 180f; De Principiis 4:1:2; Contra Celsus 2:52:3:7.
[58] Comm. on John 1:37.
[59] Contra Celsus 1:68.
[60] Contra Celsus 8:17.
[61] De Principiis 4:4:4.
[62] Contra Celsus 3:61,62.
[63] Contra Celsus 6:67.

and he became an example for us through his death and resurrection.[64]

The Continuity of the Righteousness of Jesus Christ

❖ The righteousness of Christ towards humanity was not limited to the stage of his incarnation, but his power continues to work to guide and spiritually grow those who believe in God through him even to this day.[65]

The Incarnation and the Angels

Origen believes that the mediation of the Logos does not stop at the Church, but also extends to the angels and forces. The Logos gradually works to unify all in him, without violating the freedom of rational creatures.[66][67]

The Coming of Christ Twice

Origen suggests that the two times when our Lord Jesus Christ was absent from Cana of Galilee symbolize his coming twice.

❖ The Son of Man indeed came, even if not in his glory (Origen quotes Is 2:53-5 here), for it was necessary for him to come in this way in order to "bear our sins" and suffer on our behalf, as it was not fitting for Christ in his glory to "bear our sins" and suffer for us. But he is coming again in his glory after preparing his disciples for this coming during his appearance... in his first coming he was like "our humble body" (in 21:3) when he emptied himself, took the form of a servant, and will return

---

64   *Comm. on John Frag. 14o0 on Colos. 1:18.*
65   *Contra Celsus 1:43.*
66   *De Principiis 4:4:5; 4:3:13 [left out by Rufinus; In Lev. hom. 1; Contra Celsus 7:17).*
67   *Cf. De Principiis 3:5:6-8.*

humanity to the form of God.⁶⁸ The purpose of his first coming was not to condemn humanity before teaching them and guiding them to what they should be. He did not come to punish the wicked and reward the righteous, but he came to plant in his wonderful way the seed of his word with divine authority in the human race.⁶⁹

Jesus Christ and Our Need for Salvation

1. Origen tells Salus that the only thing God seeks is the salvation of his creation, not out of need, but because of his wonderful love for his creation.⁷⁰

2. Natural ethics are not sufficient. Salvation is achieved through Christ alone, as there is no benefit in practicing good deeds before being righteous in the Lord. The human soul has reached a state of weakness and dispersion to a degree that it cannot be justified apart from the power of God and his grace in Christ.⁷¹

❖ Where the enemy spread his nets everywhere, and almost everyone was about to fall into his trap, the need for someone greater in power arose, to overcome him and pave the way for those who follow him.⁷²

Basil Studer decides that the external mission of the Logos for Origen consists of two parts: one related to creation, and the other to the history of salvation.⁷³

---

68 *Comm. on Matt. 12:29 on 16:27.*
69 *Contra Celsus 2:38.*
70 *Contra Celsus 8:62; cf. St. Clement of Alexandria: Stromata 7:14.*
71 *Comm on Rom. 8:2.*
72 *Comm. on the Songs of Songs, book 3:13 (ACW).*
73 *Basil Studer : Trinity and Incarnation, p. 80.*

❖ *The world was created, the soul of the world was established, and the system of the world was established.*[74]

❖ *He founded the work of salvation, which is based on preserving the world.*[75] *Even in his incarnation, salvation served the concept of this preservation. "We find in the history of salvation that the Logos is behind all human events."*[76] *In the Old Testament, the Lord Christ practiced the acts of prophetic vision through chosen men and through his personal appearance.*[77] *He became human in order to save humans from demons, restore the law, and present himself as an example.*[78]

❖ The completion of salvation is achieved when Christ subjected himself, as the head of the church, to the Father, so that God may be all in all.[79] This is realized at the final coming of the Logos in creation and history.[80]

The concept of salvation

The suffering Christ is the rider who rode the white horse, symbolizing the truth declared of his glory, and his garments are sprinkled with blood (Rev 19:13), which is a sign of his victory. The sacrifice of Christ was a preparation for the salvation of the Christian soul and its salvation. We can summarize Origen's concept of salvation in the following points:

1. **Salvation and Enlightenment: According to Origen, salvation cannot be separated from enlightenment. Our Savior is the divine**

---

74 *De Principiis 2:1:3; 1:2:9; i:3:5f.*
75 *Cf. De Principiis 2:6:3.*
76 *Cf. De Principiis 2:6:31.*
77 *Cf. De Principiis 1:Praef.:1.*
78 *Cf. De Principiis 3:5:6; 3:3:2.*
79 *Cf. De Principiis 1:6:1f; 3:5:6.*
80 *Cf. De Principiis 1:2:10.*

announcer, teacher, and illuminator. He expresses salvation through light in resistance to darkness, and knowledge in resistance to ignorance. Regarding the salvific work of our Lord Jesus Christ, J.N.D. Kelly[81] says, "The Logos is our teacher, who has given us the Law, and the highest example for us."[82] In connection with Him, we lose the nature of death and irrationality and become "divine life and reason." He is the "model of complete life"[83] and the example of true virtue to which Christians[84] are transformed, enabling them to become partners in the divine nature.[85] Origen says, "By appearing in bodily form and giving Himself as flesh, He calls those who are in the flesh to first transform them into the likeness of the Word who became flesh, then elevate them to see Him as He was before the incarnation."[86] Also, "With Christ, humanity and divinity are united, so that human nature can be glorified." We can say that Origen considered his God a teacher and viewed the world of God as a vast educational institution. From the words of John in his Gospel: "And the grace and truth came through Jesus Christ" (John 17:1). And that Christ is "the truth" (John 6:14), indicating that the only accepted source for Christian life is concentrated in the words of Christ and His teachings. Christ was also the effective Word of God in Moses and the prophets.[87]

❖ The Spirit that worked in the prophets was Christ. He is the one who bestowed upon us the spirit of prophecy.[88]

---

81 *See J.N.D. Kelly, page !84-5.*
82 *De princ. 4:1:2; 4:3:12; Contra Cels. 2:52;3:7.*
83 *In Joh. 1:37:268.*
84 *Contra Cels. 8:17.*
85 *De Princ. 4:4:4.*
86 *Contra Cels. 6:68.*
87 *Contra Cels. 3:28.*
88 *Sel Lam. 4:20.*

Redemption is the first aspect of enlightenment. It is a struggle in which truth confronts the forces of darkness before completely erasing them.

2. **Salvation and reconciliation with God: "We have peace with God" (Romans 1:5), through our Lord Jesus Christ who reconciled us with God through the sacrifice of His blood. Christ came to destroy the enemies, make peace, and reconcile us with the Father from whom we had separated by the barrier of evil that we erected with our sins.[89]**

3. **Salvation and the defeat of Satan: Since the moment of his birth, the life of Christ has been a struggle with the forces of darkness.[90] Its final defeat was accomplished in his sufferings and resurrection. Origen[91] cites Colossians 15:2 to prove that the death of the Savior has a dual aspect: as an example, and at the same time a crown of his victory over Satan, which was achieved on the cross with the rulers and powers. Salvation is essentially seen through the struggle between God and Satan, and between good and evil. Origen affirms that the Lord Christ, as the Logos, triumphs over opposing forces with his wisdom, wages war against his enemies with argument and righteousness, until he destroys folly and evil.[92] True doctrine leads to victory over sin.[93] The light shines not only on the darkness of human souls, but penetrates to where it lies and continues the rulers of darkness in their war against the human race. As the Lord shines upon this darkness, darkness pursues the light but does not comprehend it.[94] Young says that the defeat of Satan is actually the main subject in Origen's soteriological theology.**

---

89 *Comm. on Rom. 4:8.*
90 *Contra Celsus 1:60:6:45; hom. in Lucia. 30:31.*
91 *Hom. in Jos 8:3; in Matt 12:40.*
92 *Comm. on John 2:4.*
93 *Comm. on Rom. 6:3.*
94 *Comm. on John 2:21; Frances M. Young: The Use of Sacrificial Ideas in Greek Christian Writers from the New Testament to John Chrysostom, Philadelphia 1979, p. 174.*

In his work De Principiis, he devotes a whole chapter to "how the devil and opposing forces are at war with the human race according to the Bible."[95] The activity of demons plays a major role in Origen's dialogue with Salus,[96] and his sermons on the book of Hosea are filled with wars against Satan, because the wars of Hosea are symbols of the wars of Christ and his followers against Satan and his angels.[97] In his commentary on the Letter to the Romans,[98] Origen explains the incarnation and work of Christ, through a metaphor in which he expresses this soteriological theological position: There was a king characterized by justice and nobility, in a war against a tyrannical oppressor, and he tried to avoid the use of violence and shedding blood because some of his men were fighting in the ranks of that oppressor, and he was eager to liberate them, not to destroy them. He succeeded in persuading his men to abandon the oppressor and return to their true kingdom. In doing so, he succeeded in binding the strong, and he defeated the rulers and their forces, as well as in recovering the bodies of the prisoners who died in the war. This idea was fundamental in Origen's concept of salvation, and the theory on which he bases his explanation of all soteriological theological problems.[99]

4. **Salvation and obedience to the divine teacher:** Frances Young says that salvation theology for Origen includes another important theme related to the idea of Christ as a teacher, and that is to practice obedience to him as the way. This is especially clear during the call to martyrdom, which is the peak of commitment. Those who follow Christ, especially

---

95 *De Principiis 3:2; also 1:5:1; 3:3:6; 3:5:6.*
96 *Contra Celsus 8:55-57, etc.; also 1:31; 6:43; 7:17; 8:44,54.*
97 *Hom. on Jos. 12:1; 7:3-6,7; 9:4,5.*
98 *Comm. on Rom. 5:10; also 5:1,3,6,7,10; 4:8.*
99 *Frances M. Young: The Use of Sacrificial Ideas in Greek Christian Writers from the New Testament to John Chrysostom, Philadelphia 1979, p. 173 ff.*

in martyrdom, have the Lord reveal to them what they did not understand before, as they grasp all the mysteries and secrets that pertain to truth. The martyrs in Christ break the forces of evil, and they triumph with him by participating in his sufferings and in the great achievements accomplished through his sufferings, so we quickly see the forces of evil defeated and humiliated in disgrace.[100] Obedience, self-denial, and humility are also a mimicry of Christ. They are part of the salvific teaching work, leading to virtue and participation in the divine nature, repairing what is corrupted, which is the work of Christ.[101]

5. Salvation and healing from the slavery of corruption: Salvation is a healing process carried out by the true physician and at the same time is the remedy. Christ grants healing to those sick with sin. He came to our death to save humanity from the slavery of corruption. This is also part of Christ's victory over the power of death, sin, and the devil.[102]

❖ *Come now to Jesus, the heavenly physician. Enter into this clinic, which is his church. Look, there lie many of the weak. You find a woman seeking purification (Mark 25:5; Luke 12), as well as lepers isolated "outside the camp" because of the defilement of their leprosy (Mark 40:1, Luke 46:13). They seek healing from the physician, asking how they can become healthy and how they can be cleansed. Jesus the physician is himself the Word of God, preparing the medicine for his patients, not from herbal remedies, but from the sanctity of words. The medicine for souls is in Christ, so surely it will be understood from these books read in the church, how everyone must gather useful herbs from the fields and*

---

100 *Exhortation of Martyrdom 42.*
101 *De Principiis 3:5:6; Frances M. Young, p. 175.*
102 *Comm. on John 1:25,28, 35; 2:6; 10:4.*

mountains, meaning the power of words, so that the one who is sick in soul may be healed, not by the power of external branches (of medicinal plants) and superficial bark, but by the effective essence.[103]

6. **Salvation and enjoying redemption: The work of redemption begins in Origen's thought by uprooting the evil forces, death, and sin that oppress human nature, followed by reconciliation of human nature with God.**

   ❖ *No one can die with Jesus who died so that we may live. Everyone has sinned and needed another to die for them, not for them to die for others.*[104] *This description reflects the work of the Lord Christ in his symbolic interpretation of the rituals of the Day of Atonement as mentioned in Leviticus 16. They would present two goats before the Lord at the entrance of the temple (Leviticus 7:16), symbolizing Barabbas and Jesus. Pilate released Barabbas alive with the sins of the people upon his head. While Jesus was presented as a sin offering, to cover the sins of those deserving forgiveness. The wilderness to which the redemption ram was sent was a place devoid of virtues, devoid of God, devoid of justice, devoid of Christ, and devoid of anything good. The one who released the redemption ram into the wilderness had to be purified. It must be understood that he represents the Lord himself, our Savior. Origen draws a comparison between the two tasks. He first points out that just as a man washes his clothes in the evening, so did Christ cleanse (cover) our body and blood, meaning the human nature he took from us. Then he interprets the pulling out of the redemption ram in Paul's language in Colossians 15:2, on the cross stripping the rulers and authorities, triumphing over them openly in it. Origen affirms*

---

103   *Homilies on Leviticus 8:1 (See Frs. of the Church)*
104   *Comm. Ser. Matt. 88 on 26:33-35.*

that Christ expelled the hordes of evil spirits and rulers of darkness in this world, triumphing over them. No one else had the power to cast them into the desolate wilderness, meaning into hell. And when he returned after completing his work, he ascended to heaven, where he completed his purification on the heavenly altar, to present a covenant for our body he took with him in purity. This was the "atonement death," where God forgives humans when sin is erased, hostile forces are removed, and human nature is purified, then reconciliation with God is achieved.[105]*

7. **Salvation and exaltation in Christ our God: For Origen, the atoning death of Christ was given to humanity to escape the control of evil forces and to partake in the divine nature.[106]**

   ❖ *The theology of Christ came from above, and through it, this fire was ignited, so it became fitting for the heavenly fire to ignite all those things that were done in the flesh by the Savior, and for everything to return to the nature of divinity. Truly, the burnt offering sacrifice united in his body, offered through the cross, the earthly with the heavenly, the human with the divine.[107]*

   ❖ *For the ancients, they used to slaughter sheep, goats, cattle, and birds... But for you, the Son of God was sacrificed. So how can you continue to delight in sin after that? ... You have heard about the number of sacrifices that were offered for sins in the Law. Now hear about the abundance of forgiveness for sins in the Gospel.[108]*

8. **Salvation and glorification of believers: During the resur-**

---

105   *In Lev. Hom. 10:2.*
106   *De Principiis 4:4:4; Frances M. Young, p. 184.*
107   *In Lev. hom. 1:5 (cf. G.W. Barkley - Frs. of the Church).*
108   *In Lev. hom. 2:4 (cf. G.W. Barkley - Frs. of the Church).*

rection of Christ, believers taste the pledge of the glory of the resurrection. In His resurrection, the humanity of Christ was glorified. And as the church, it is our right to be glorified through unity with Him. The resurrection of Christ is an example of the glorification of believers.

> ❖ *In order to grant us the blessings of being born in Christ, He became the firstborn among the dead, so that He might have the preeminence in all things. As believers, we are taken by His resurrection as His first fruits. Truly, if we hold fast to the grace of these blessings until the end, the mercy of our Lord Jesus Christ Himself will support us.*[109]

The death of Christ as an atoning sacrifice

Origen uses what Isaiah 53 prophesied about the sufferings of Christ, saying: "He bore our sorrows, and He was crushed for our iniquities, our discipline was upon Him, so that we may be disciplined and obtain peace." In certain paragraphs, Origen decides that the death of Christ is understood as Him paying His precious blood to the devil, whom we sold ourselves to, so that when the devil thinks he has obtained the price by accepting Christ instead of humanity, he is then crucified and loses his power.[110]

> ❖ *As the victim, He shed His blood as an atonement for the forgiveness of past sins. This atonement is obtained by every believer through their faith. Surely, atonement was achieved by the shedding of the holy blood (Hebrews 9:22).*[111]
>
> ❖ *Christ died for us, how? By bearing the sins of the world. He bore our weaknesses, and suffered for us ... Jesus alone*

---

109 *Homily on Numbers [3:4]: Drewery 132.*
110 *In Joh. 28:19:165.*
111 *Comm. on Rom. 3:8 on 3:25.*

redeemed the whole world "who, being in the form of God, did not consider it robbery to be equal with God (the Father), but made Himself of no reputation, taking the form of a servant", and was offered as a sacrifice for the whole world.[112]

❖ *Truly, Christ did not commit sin, but He "became sin on our behalf", when He descended while in the form of God, to become "in the form of a servant". When He died while not subject to death. And suffered while not susceptible to pain. And was seen while not visible. And because the judgment of death and all the weaknesses of the body have come upon us due to our wrong condition, Christ, who took on the form of man and was present in His likeness, was offered as a sacrifice to God like a lamb without blemish, that is, His body without sin, as a substitute for the sin He took upon Himself from us, "bearing our sins".*[113]

Origen believes that the words indicating atonement were never intended to mean the appeasement of the divine wrath of the Father. One of the problems he and his contemporaries faced was the challenge posed by the views of Marcionists who claimed that Christ was announced as the God of love, while the God of the Old Covenant was the God of justice and wrath, distinguishing Him from Jesus Christ. For this reason, Origen may have been forced to clarify the wrath of God in many of his sermons.[114] Origen speaks of Jesus[115] who offered Himself or His life as a redemption for many. To whom did He offer it? In his opinion, it was not doubtlessly for the Father, but rather for the devil who had control over us, until Jesus Himself was given as a substitute for us. He offered Himself in exchange for the souls of humans that the devil demanded as a debt to be paid.[116] The devil accepted this

---

112 *Comm. on Rom. 4:11; see Frances M. Young, p. 182-3.*
113 *In Lev. hom. 3:1.*
114 *Frances M. Young, p. 185 ff.*
115 *In Matt. 16:8; 12:28; In Joh. 6:53:274; Hom. In Exod. 6:9; etc.*
116 *Comm. on Matt. 16:8; Young, p. 183.*

exchange, but he could not hold onto Jesus in his grasp, which proved that He was stronger than death, and thus deprived him of his victim. The devil was deceived, thinking he could prevail over Jesus, failing to realize that he could not bear the torment of holding Him. Thus, the life that was offered as a sacrifice, and the blood that was shed as atonement - in Origen's opinion - served as a ransom paid by God to the devil. The Holy Father "did not spare His only Son, but gave Him up for all of us," like the burden of God who dies for every human to bear the sin of the world.[117]

> ❖ *In any case, the sin of all was not erased by the burden, unless He bore the pains and sufferings for the sinners. Not only were the thorns scattered, but they were deeply embedded in the hands of every person intoxicated by evil, losing the strength to awaken from their sin.*[118]

The Sacrifice of Christ and Animal Sacrifices

In his letter to the Hebrews, Saint Paul clearly explained the difference between animal sacrifices and the sacrifice of Christ. The former was repeated due to its weakness and inadequacy in renewing the depth of human nature. The latter was presented only once, as it still has the power to renew our inner selves. Origen explained that animal sacrifices were consumed by eating or burning. As for the sacrifice of God, it is not only living, but also gives life to those who partake in it. Jesus Christ - the priest and the sacrifice at the same time - did not offer animal blood to be consumed, but His blood that gives life, resurrection, and eternity. He continually changes those who believe in Him from submission to death to immortality, and saves their nature so they become partners in His life and bear His likeness.

---

[117] *Contra Cells 8:43; Frances M. Young, p. 183-4.*
[118] *Comm. on John 6:55.*

The Sacrifice of Christ for Sin.[119]

In the Old Covenant, they used to try to erase sins with the blood of bulls and goats, but they did not succeed in doing so. The Son of God came in the likeness of sinful flesh. He condemned sin in the flesh, becoming a sacrifice for sin, and was offered for purification from sin. Origen does not pose a question regarding the principle, as the entire Old Covenant testifies to it. As we have seen, the idea of erasing sin was Origen's concept during atonement, and as in the New Covenant, the linguistic terms of atonement were used in this context. On certain occasions, Origen tries to explain how the sacrifice of Christ can erase sin. As seen in the Book of Leviticus, the priests would eat the offerings for sin. Therefore - as Origen says - Christ, as both priest and sacrifice at the same time, would eat the sins of the people. God is a consuming fire. God the fiery one consumes the sins of humanity. He takes them upon himself, devours them, and purifies us. Therefore, Christ took our sins upon himself, and as a fire, he consumed and devoured them with himself. In another interpretation heavily relying on Old Covenant ideas, Christ was a flawless offering. And because of this purity, in a way, anyone who touches the flesh of that sacrifice becomes sanctified. All of these attempts at interpretation rely on accepting the language and ideas of the Bible to confirm the reality that the sacrifice dealt with sin in a way that it would be removed, but it does not explain adequately how that is done.

Whenever Origen needed to explain something, he would resort to traditional theory, such as his statement:

❖ *The slaughtered lamb was made, for certain hidden reasons, a purification and cleansing for the whole world. Therefore, out of God's love for humans, he surrendered to death, restoring us with his blood, from the one who had taken us by force, being sold by our sins.*

---

119   Frances M. Young, p. 179.

The nature of the sacrifice offered by Christ.

The sacrifice of Christ surpasses the sacrifices of the Old Covenant, as it takes place in heaven.[120] Origen looks to the sacrifice of Christ on earth,[121] his death on the cross, as a symbol of his heavenly sacrifice. However, he presents a completely different distinction between them. Just as the priest in the past would offer one bull on the altar as a burnt offering, and then offer another as a sin offering to be burned outside the burnt offering, there is a difference between the burnt offering and the sin offering. As a figurative interpretation, Christ offered a burnt offering on the heavenly altar. As for on earth, outside the heavenly burnt offering, where sin has reigned since the days of Adam, he offered it for sin. Origen perhaps considers the heavenly offering of Christ as a gift, a sacrifice of glorification, worship, and thanksgiving (in the name of the Church). Origen often refers to the sacrifice of Christ as the complete worship and obedience to the Father, the example that Christians are committed to imitating.[122]

> ❖ *Therefore, consider whether it is possible that Jesus, of whom Paul said, through his blood "made peace, not only with earthly things, but also with those in heaven," is the same sacrifice that was offered in heaven, not for sin certainly, but as an offering. As for on earth "where sin reigned from Adam to Moses, he was offered "for sin," the one who suffered "outside the camp," outside that camp which Jacob saw, I think, when he said: "How awesome is this place! This is none other than the house of God; this is the gate of heaven" (Gen 28:17). Outside this heavenly camp is where we live, this earthly place where Christ suffered in the flesh.*[123]

---

120   *In Lev. hom. 1:3.*
121   *In Lev. hom 1:3:3.*
122   Frances M. Young, p. 215.
123   *In Lev. 1:3:3 (Barkley).*

Christ is the great High Priest.

The expression of Saint Cyril of Alexandria "Christ is the altar, the sacrifice, and the priest"[124] is taken from Origen.[125]

> ❖ *The fact that Isaac carried the wood of the burnt offering symbolizes Christ carrying his cross. And if carrying the wood of the burnt offering is the task of the priest, then Christ is indeed both the sacrifice and the priest.*[126]

Not only do the sacrifices of the Old Covenant point to Christ, but in Christ, the shadows and images of the great High Priest are fulfilled. In his role as the great High Priest, he offers a true sacrifice to the Father, he himself is the sacrifice, through which he appeases the Father.[127]

> ❖ *Because there is no righteous person except one, and that is God (Matthew 17:19), likewise among rivers there is no righteous river except the Jordan, and no other river can cleanse from leprosy. So, only the one who has faith in washing himself in Jesus (the Jordan) can be cleansed. I think this is the reason why the Israelites wept when they sat on the banks of the rivers of Babylon, and remembered Zion. Those who were exiled because of their wickedness, when they tasted other waters after the holy waters of the Jordan, longed for the river of their salvation. They sat by the rivers of Babylon, unable to stand any longer, so they wept. Just as Jeremiah*

---

124 *PG 68:596-604.*
125 *Jean Daniélou: The Bible and the Liturgy, Michigan 1979, p. 130 n.*
126 *In Gen. hom. 8:1.*
127 *In Rom. 3:8.*

rebuked those who desired to drink from the waters of Egypt, ignoring the water that comes down from heaven, hence its name became "the one that descends down," the Jordan.[128]

Origen interprets the death of Christ as an act of substitution or as an atoning sacrifice. He argues that Jesus, as the leader of the Church, is the head of a body of which we are members. He took our sins upon himself and bore them, and bore our pains by his will. As a true priest, he offered a true sacrifice to the Father, he himself is the sacrifice, presenting the offerings of Christians of compassion, justice, piety, and peace, presenting the lives of believers that have been transformed.[129][130][131]

❖ *Christ is the great high priest who, with his blood, made God have compassion on you, and reconciled with you in the Father.*[132]

The mystery of the cross.

Henry de Lubac says: The announcement that the crucified Christ has his fundamental importance remains; because "the management of pain" is the center. It is the undisputed "management." Origen teaches that the sin of sin cannot be healed without the cross. And that the blood of Christ saved the church as a whole, without distinction between classes. It is also taught that the death of Christ is the tree of life for all of us. And all the fruits come from this death, like a grain of wheat that must fall to the ground and appear as if it were lost. And it is announced that all the glory and wealth of the church is centered in

---

128 *Comm. on John, book 6:28.*
129 *Hom. in Lev. 1:3.*
130 *In Lev. hom 9:6.*
131 *Comm. on Rom. 4:8.*
132 *In Leviticum hom. 9:10.*

the pains of Christ. In order for man to be guided, he has no choice but to "come to the cross of Christ." And that the wisdom of the complete man comes not from any other knowledge than meditation "on the deep mysteries revealed to us by Paul", then in rejecting the wisdom of the world... There is no escape from being crucified for the wisdom of this world, where there is complete contradiction between the narrow path to salvation, as shown to us in the cross of Christ, and the wide and easy path that the wise men of this world seek to occupy us with. The vision of the Logos can only be acquired by paying the price of death to the world and the cost of severe trials. And no matter how much this vision is fused, it will not make us lose the image of Jesus crucified, who is at the same time the priest and the sacrifice. There is no wisdom that exempts us from carrying his cross and following him. And even with the assumption, as Paul did, that we were caught up to the third heaven, there is no avoiding falling again, except by carrying the cross and following Jesus, in whom we find our greatest priest who passed through to the heavens.[133]

- ❖ *Every soul comes to childhood, and is on its way to full maturity, and even until the fullness of time it is in need of a trainer, agents, and guardians. And after all this, the believer accepts (as a child under guardianship) without any difference from the slave, even though he is the owner of all (Galatians 1:4-2) when he is liberated from the trainer, agents, and guardians, making the inheritance that is in accordance with the priceless pearl, which, when obtained, makes up for the details, and one becomes able to accept the "grace of knowing Christ" (Ephesians 8:3).*[134]

- ❖ *The pains of the cross were a judgment for this whole world. That divine event on the cross included the judgment of all present*

---

133   *Henri De Lubac: Origen, On First Principles, NY., 1966 (Koetschau text together with an introduction and notes by G.W. Butterworth, p. XX.*
134   *Comm. on Matt., book 2:9.*

> *things, making him say when the moment of pain approached, "Now the judgment of this world has come."*[135]

R. Cadiou decides that Origenus tells his disciples that through studying the crucified Jesus, one can reach the highest levels of spiritual life. However, he warns them of their inability to comprehend the mystery of the Savior's pains, leading them to a knowledge of Christ far from perfection. It is a mystery so difficult that even the apostles needed guidance on its meaning before they could understand it and realize that it meant our salvation. Cadiou also says that we do not need to feel ashamed of the Savior's pains, as they stem from his voluntary sacrifice and his great desire to serve. "So let us not hesitate to say that the goodness of Christ is revealed in the light of the greatest and most theological conformity to the image of the Father as he puts himself." His acceptance of servitude was not just a small part of his sacrifice. He embodied the incarnate Word in his pains, silence, and sufferings, and in all the sorrows that afflict the human heart. And although his authority over them was limited due to his sinlessness, his suffering was complete, as the Savior always desired it to be, even with his majesty and divinity. He remained silent before Pilate because "he desired to suffer for humanity. If he had spoken, he would not have been crucified in weakness.[136][137]

The cross is a symbol of divine love and victory over the devil

> ❖ *Everything that happened was only because of his unlimited love for us. This is true whether it concerns our Lord Jesus Christ in his death for the wicked, or God the Father in giving his only Son as redemption for sinners.*[138]

---

135 *Comm. on John frag 89 on 12:31.*
136 *R. Cadiou: Origen, Herder Book Co., 1944, p. 301.*
137 *In Joan. 19:2 PG 14:544; R. Cadiou: Origen, Herder Book Co., 1944.*
138 *Comm. on Rom. 6:10 on 5:6f.*

The cross gives believers a complete example of how a Christian sacrifices himself to death for God.

❖ **Christ slaughtered enmity in his body, as in his death he set an example for humanity that the war against sin is to be fought to the death. And finally, by settling enmity in his body, his blood reconciled humanity with God.**[139]

❖ *It is reasonable that one who becomes a living model for humanity shows them how to die for their faith in divine truth.*[140]

The cross is a symbol of victory

❖ *When pagans led their enemies in victory processions, they displayed a cross symbolizing triumph over their heads. In this way, we see the cross as a symbol of victory over the devil. Therefore, Paul says, "Far be it from me to boast except in the cross of our Lord Jesus Christ" (Galatians 6:14). He teaches how the cross can free me from evil when I embrace it through the death of Christ to save me from death.*[141]

❖ *What do demons fear? And what do they tremble at? Without dispute, it is the cross in which they were "triumphed over" (Colossians 2:15). Therefore, fear and terror come upon them when they see the sign of the cross, which is established in faith.*[142]

In Origen's commentary on what is mentioned in the book of Joshua (Joshua 8:29 LXX) "Hang the king of Ai on a double tree," he says: [The cross of our Lord Jesus Christ was double. That is, he stood on two supports. For outwardly the Son of God was crucified in the flesh,

---

139 *Comm. on Rom. 6:12.*
140 *Contra Celsus 2:16.*
141 *Comm. on Cor. 6.*
142 *In Exod. hom. 6:8.*

and in secret the devil was nailed to that cross with his principalities and powers (Colossians 2:14, 15). Therefore, there are two meanings to the cross: the first mentioned by the Apostle Peter that the crucified Christ "left us an example" (1 Peter 2:21). And the second is that it is a sign of victory over the devil who was crucified on it and was defeated.][143]

The cross unites believers from all over the world in the unity of love. [When lifted up on the cross, he embraced the whole world between his arms.][144]

Jesus Christ is our sufficiency.

Christ as the satisfier of souls: Man needs the word of God, as the Savior who restores the soul of man to its original nature and satisfies all the needs of man.

❖ *The Apostle says to those whose senses have been trained to distinguish between good and evil (Hebrews 5:14). Christ became all of these things, to correspond with the different senses of the soul. The true light was called, so you find the eyes of the soul enlightened. He (the Logos) so you find its ears hearing something. He is the bread of life so you find the soul tasting something. In the same way, he was called by the nard or the ointment, so that the sense of smell in the soul can perceive the sweet smell of the word. For the same reason, it is also said that he can be felt and touched, and he was called the incarnate Logos, so that the inner hand of the soul can touch him in relation to the word of life (John 4:1). But all these things are one, the word of God himself, who adapts to the different emotions of prayer, according to those multiple*

---

143 *In Josh. hom. 8:3 on 8:29.*
144 *In Exod. hom. 11:4 on Isa. 65:2.*

designations, so that none of the capacities of the soul are left empty of his grace.[145]

Christ presents himself to those who feel they are in need of him. This feeling gives them the right to dwell in their hearts.

❖ *Truly, I can say that he becomes everything that every creature in need of liberation needs. Therefore, he becomes the light of the people if they are in the darkness of evil seeking that light that shines in the darkness that they do not comprehend. He does not become a light to the people if they are not in darkness.*[146]

❖ *There are different images of the Logos, in his appearance to everyone who knows him according to the situation of each of them, whether they are at their beginning, or have made some progress, small or large, or those who are close to realizing virtue or those who have already acquired it.*[147]

❖ *Christ is present in each individual according to the degree allowed by his merit.*[148]

Titles of Christ

❖ *Holding on to Jesus is holding on to the Logos, wisdom, righteousness, and the power of the Father, for Christ is all of that.*[149]

---

145   *Comm. On Song of Songs, book 2:9.*
146   *Comm. On John 1:20.*
147   *Contra Celsus 2:16.*
148   *De Principiis 4:4:2.*
149   *Comm. on John 32:31.*

His sufficiency for beginners and spiritually mature individuals

Origen distinguishes between the titles of Christ, those presented to beginners and those presented to those who have matured spiritually. The first group needs Christ the physician to heal their wounded nature, the shepherd to care for their needs, and the savior who forgives their sins, while others need him as wisdom, Logos, and righteousness.

❖ *Truly blessed are those who, in their need for the Son of God, have surpassed the need for him as a physician to heal their diseases or as a shepherd or benefactor, and their need for him has become like wisdom, Logos, and righteousness, or one of the other titles he offers to those whose maturity allows them to deserve his most noble blessings.*[150]

Christ is all goodness

❖ *Let us contemplate what the Gospels say in the light of the promises of goodness. We must say that the goodness announced by the apostles in these Gospels is simply: Jesus. One of the goodness they announce is the resurrection. But the resurrection, in essence, is Jesus, as he says: "I am the resurrection." And as Isaiah says: "How beautiful on the mountains are the feet of those who bring good news" (Isaiah 7:52). He sees how beautiful and fitting it is for the messengers who walked (in Christ), saying: "I am the way." They praise the feet of those walking in the intellectual path of Jesus Christ, and they go through this door to God.*[151]

---

150   *Comm. on John 1:20.*
151   *Comm. on John, 1:10.*

Christ is the beginning and the end

❖ *The Beginning and the End, an expression we always apply to something that represents a complete unity. The beginning of any house is the foundation, and its end is the roof barrier. There is no escape from thinking in this framework, for Christ is the cornerstone of the great unity, of the body that He saves. Christ, the only Son, is all and in all. He is the beginning in the man who took on His form, and He is present as the end in the last of the saints, as well as present for those who are between this and that. He is present as the beginning in Adam, and the end in his life on earth, according to the saying: "The last Adam became a life-giving spirit." This saying is in harmony with the interpretation we have presented of the beginning and the end.*[152]

The Christ Logos

He is the Word, as He is the interpreter of the mysteries of the divine mind, that is, He is the way to inspiration.[153]

Origen uses the term "Logos" as a source of our thinking.

❖ **Through His activity in enlightening the world, which is His light, Christ is called the "Light of the World." And through His sacrifice for those who sincerely attach themselves to Him, laying down their lives so that they may rise again renewed, He is called "the Resurrection." Through other activities, He is said to be the shepherd, the teacher, the king, the chosen pillar, and the servant. Additionally, He is the Paraclete and the Comforter. In the same manner, He is called "Logos," because He distances us from all that is irrational, trans-**

---

152   *Comm. on John 1:34 (ANF).*
153   *Charles Bigg: The Christian Platonists of Alexandria, Oxford 1913, p. 209.*

forming us into rational beings, so that we do all things, even eating and drinking, for the glory of God, driven by the Logos towards the glory of God in the ordinary actions of life and in those belonging to a more advanced stage.[154]

Christ is the Light

❖ *He Himself is the Light of the World, which also illuminates the Church with His light. Just as the moon derives its light from the sun to illuminate the night, so it is in the Church. By receiving the light of Christ, everyone living in the darkness of ignorance is enlightened. But if someone makes progress to the point where he is called "a son of the day" because he "walks properly as in the day" (Romans 13:13), "as a son of the day and a son of the light" (1 Thessalonians 5:5), this person shines with Christ, just as the day shines with the sun.*[155]

Christ is the Truth

❖ *The only Son is the Truth, because He is in solidarity with Himself, according to the will of the Father, with every mind, where all things are in complete clarity. And because He is the Truth, He is connected to every creature, each according to its merit.*[156]

Christ is the Wisdom of God.

Basil Studer says, for Origen the Son is the Wisdom, as well as the Logos or the Word. He is the Wisdom in relation to the Father. As for

---

154 *Comm. on John, book 1:42.*
155 *In Gen. hom. 1:5.*
156 *In Joan 1:27 PG 14:73; R. Cadiou: Origen, Herder Book Co., 1944, p. 176.*

the world, he is the Logos,[157] because he conveys to it the knowledge of the Father.[158]

Christ is the Way

❖ *There is nothing better than entrusting oneself into the hands of the Almighty God, and dedicating oneself to the teaching that instructs us to leave behind all that is created, and leads us to the Almighty God through the living Logos, the immutable.*[159]

Christ the King

❖ *Both the Son of God and those against Christ desire to rule. However, those against Christ want to rule in order to destroy, while Christ wants to rule in order to save humanity. Christ reigns over those who are faithful to his word, wisdom, justice, and righteousness. But if we prefer our desires over God, then sin is what rules over us, as the apostle says: "Do not let sin reign in your mortal body" (Romans 6:12). There are two kings seeking dominion: either sin or the devil who rule over the wicked, or justice and Christ who rule over the righteous. Our Lord and Savior undoubtedly desires to reign with justice, righteousness, and all virtues. He does not desire to be crowned as a king without the possibility of suffering (the cross).*[160]

---

157 *De Principiis* 1:2:2.
158 *De Principiis* 1:2:3; Basil Studer: *Trinity and Incarnation*, p. 80.
159 *Contra Celsus* 3:81.
160 *In Luc. hom.* 30:1-3.

Christ is our Kingdom

Our goal is to attain the kingdom of God within us, which is Christ himself. Origen says that Jesus is the kingdom in person. In his commentary on the Gospel of Matthew (14:12), Origen explains that the kingdom of heaven is "virtues" in their entirety, and that Christ is every virtue and all virtues together.[161]

> ❖ *He speaks of himself as the kingdom of God, for he is the king and God.*[162]

> ❖ *As long as Jesus Christ, the divine Word, who was with the Father from the beginning, does not dwell in a soul, the kingdom of heaven is not in that soul. But when a person becomes ready to receive the Word, the kingdom of heaven is within reach.*[163]

Christ the Heavenly Bread

> ❖ *The book says: "And in the morning you shall be filled with bread" (Exodus 12:16). The word of God is also bread for us, as He is "the bread of God that comes down from heaven and gives life to the world" (John 6:33, 51). But the truth of saying that this bread was given "in the morning", while we say that His coming in the flesh happened in the evening, can be understood as follows: The Lord came in the evening of the decaying world, near the end of its course. But His coming, as the "sun of righteousness" (Malachi 4:2 LXX; 20:3), has brought a new day to those who believe in Him. This is because a new light of knowledge has shone in the world, making His day "morning" by some means. The sun of*

---

161 *Comm on Matt. 14:7; Michael Green: Evangelism in the Early Church, p. 51.*
162 *In Luke hom. 32 on 10:9.*
163 *Comm. on Matt. 10:14 on 13:52.*

righteousness came with its own morning, in which those who accept His commandments are filled with bread. In addition to this interpretation, we can also understand it as the morning and the beginning of the day for each person, the beginning of our enlightenment and approach to the light of faith. Therefore, at this time, when we are still in the early stages, we cannot eat from the body of the Word, as we are not yet able to grasp the complete and full teaching. But, after long training and great progress, when we approach the evening and are pushed towards the goal of perfection, we will finally be able to comprehend the food (the strong) and the complete Word. So let us hasten to accept the heavenly grace, which gives to each mouth the taste it desires. Let us also listen to what the Lord says to those who draw near to Him: "As you have believed, so let it be done for you" (Matthew 13:8).[164] *Therefore, if you accept the word of God that you hear in the church with full faith and strength, this word will be to you as you long for it. If you are sad, He comforts you by saying: "The broken and crushed heart, God will not despise" (Psalm 17:50). And if you are joyful, hoping for the future, your joy will increase when you hear: "Rejoice in the Lord and be glad, you righteous" (Psalm 11:32). If you are angry, you will calm down when you hear: "Refrain from anger and turn from wrath" (Psalm 8:37). And if you are in pain, you will be healed when you hear: "The Lord heals all your diseases" (Psalm 103:3). If you are crushed by poverty, you will be comforted when you hear: "The Lord sustains the poor from the dust, and lifts the needy from the ash heap" (Psalm 113:7). So the*

---

164   *(Cf. Origen Comm. Matt.., Ser. 100 where he relates the differing tastes of the manna to Wis 16.20-21. It was a common Rabbinical tradition that the manna had the particular taste that each person eating it wished (Mekilta de-Rabbi Ishmael, Vayassa' ch. V; Midrach Rabbah, Exod. 25.3; Yoma 75a.)*

grace that the word of God gives you will be in your mouth with the taste you desire.[165]

❖ *What nourishes the soul but the word, and what is more precious to the mind than the wisdom of God!*[166]

Christ as a servant.

❖ *Once again, let one contemplate how Jesus' attitude was towards his disciples. He was not like one who sits at the table, but like one who serves. How, being the Son of God, he took the form of a servant to liberate those enslaved by sin, and did not hesitate when the Father addressed him: "You are my servant" (Isaiah 49). Shortly after, he says: "It is a small thing that you should be my servant" (Isaiah 6). Therefore, we do not hesitate to say that the righteousness of Christ appears in a greater and more glorious light and closer to the image of the Father, because he "humbled himself and became obedient to the point of death, even the death of the cross" (Philippians 2:8).*[167]

Christ, our hidden treasure

❖ *Heavenly matters, even the kingdom of heaven or Christ himself the king of ages, are all part of the kingdom of the heavens likened to a treasure "hidden in a field" (Matthew 13:44).*[168]

❖ *Compare the words "where all the treasures of wisdom and knowledge are hidden" (Colossians 3:2). Those treasures are*

---

165 *In Exodus hom. 7:8 (Cf. Ronad E Heine- Frs. of the Church, vol. 71.)*
166 *On Prayer 27:2.*
167 *Comm. on John, book 1:37.*
168 *Comm. on John, book 1:40.*

in Christ. From him comes "the wind" with various kinds of talents: for some wisdom talents, for others knowledge talents or faith talents, and for others any of God's gifts (1 Corinthians 12).[169]

Christ, the sun of righteousness

Origen in his commentary on the sun standing still over Gibeon in the days of Joshua, to avenge the people from their enemies (Joshua 10:12-14), says that it was a symbol of the work of our Savior who turns our lives into an extended day until we achieve the final victory over the enemy.

- ❖ *We would like to explain, if possible, how Jesus spreads light and lengthens the day for the salvation of our souls and the destruction of the forces of evil. The sun always rises and is never overtaken by darkness, that is the sun of righteousness that shines with the light of truth in the hearts of believers. And when the number of believers is complete, evil comes in the last generation where the love of many grows cold due to increased selfishness and lack of righteousness. Then only a few believers will remain, "and the days will be shortened" (Matthew 24:22). Yes, only God knows the length of the day at the time of salvation, and shortens time during trials and tribulations. For us, let us walk in fear throughout the light of the day, performing the works of light, as long as we have the day, and the time of light extends to us.*[170]

- ❖ *Let us fight our enemies "we wrestle against principalities, against powers, against the rulers of the darkness of this age, against spiritual hosts of wickedness in the heavenly places" (Ephesians 6:12). The sun of righteousness will not cease to*

---

169   *In Jer. hom. 8:5 on 10:3.*
170   *In Jos. hom. 10:3.*

accompany us, for he will not leave us. He is not in a hurry to set, for as he says: "Lo, I am with you always" (Matthew 28:20). He is not with us only in times of distress, but all days, until the end of the age, until we overcome our enemies (the demons).[171]

Christ is the source of true joy

❖ *God's word does not show His beauty, but rather He shows the healing of the sick, as well as His concern for alleviating drought, to bring joy to those who are healthy and able to join the banquet.*[172]

Christ protect us

❖ *We live under the grace of Christ.*[173]

❖ *The Christ is the rock.*[174]

Christ, the source of salvation.

❖ *No one boasts of their victory or attributes it to their personal bravery, but because they know that Jesus is the giver of victory "Let no one boast" (Jeremiah 21:10). The apostle understood this when he said: "Not I, but the grace of God with me" (1 Corinthians 10:15). May God guide me (after my victory in the battle of life). I do not attribute my victory to any merit of mine, but to His cross.*[175]

---

171 *In Jos. hom. 10:5.*
172 *Comm. on John, book 10:10.*
173 *Sel Lament. 4:20.*
174 *Fr. Malaty: Luke, p. 358.*
175 *In Jos. hom 12:2.*

❖ *Jesus, He is the one who eradicates the vices within us, and brings down the kingdoms of evil with corruption.*[176]

Christ is the comfort of our souls.

❖ *The book does not say, "and the land rested from war" in the days of Moses, but in the days of Joshua (Joshua 23:11). It is certain that our "territory" of our own lives, I mean the field of our struggles and trials, will not rest from war except by the power of Jesus. Because what is inside us are tribes of vices that besiege the soul.*[177]

Christ is the bridegroom of the soul.

❖ *Christ is called the bridegroom of the soul, to whom the soul is united when it comes to faith.*[178]

Christ and the explanation of the secret of the book.

❖ *He is the one who "explains the scriptures" (Luke 24:32), and thus he sets the hearts of the disciples on fire.*[179]

The prophets and the Lord Christ.

Origen believes that many prophets accepted the grace of Christ when they desired to see him through their knowledge of symbolism.

---

176   In Josh. 15:4.
177   In Josh. Hom. 1:7.
178   In Gen. Hom. 10:4.
179   In Exod. hom. 12:4.

The Christ and the Spirit of Prophecy.

❖ *Christ is the one who bestowed upon us the spirit of prophecy.*[180]

Let us carry Jesus Christ.

Simon the Elder reveals humanity's need to enter into the temple of the Lord under the guidance of the Holy Spirit, carrying Jesus Christ in their hands, until they are released from the prison of this world.

- *Simon did not enter the temple by chance, but he was led by the Spirit of God to it. If you also want to accept Christ, and embrace Him in your hands, then be ready to leave the prison, so that the Spirit may lead you to enter.*

The structure of the Lord, for Christ is inside the church, in the temple that is built of living stones.[181]

❖ *Send the word its rays that reach the souls of those willing to receive it.*[182]

❖ *By His power, in which He emptied Himself, He also grew. He began as weak, taking on a weak body, then grew stronger. The Son of God emptied Himself, and with the same power He was filled with wisdom, and the grace of God was with Him.*[183]

❖ *Saint Mary and Saint Joseph sought Jesus Christ among relatives and friends, but they did not find Him. We do not find Jesus among relatives and friends according to the flesh. We do not find Him in the family according to the flesh. I do not find my Jesus among the crowds, but I seek Him in the temple of God, I seek Him in the church, I seek Him among*

---

180   *Sel. Lam. 4:20.*
181   *In Luc. hom. 15:3.*
182   *Contra Celsus 6:79.*
183   *In Luc. hom. 19:2.*

> *the teachers who frequent the temple, there I find Him. Let us seek Him with great effort, seeking Him in affliction, for we will find Him, as the scripture says: "Behold, your father and I have been looking for you in affliction" (Luke 48:2). Do not seek Him with weakness, laziness, and hesitation, as some do and do not find Him.*[184]

- ❖ *If one day you lose the Son of God, seek Him first in the temple. Hurry to the temple, there you will find Jesus, the Word and Wisdom.*[185]

He is the way and the door.

- ❖ Since no one can be with the Father without first ascending to the divinity of the Son, through whom he receives the blessing of the Father, the Savior is described in the Holy Scriptures as "the door" and "the way" that leads to the truth, and He is the Savior. He says: "I am the way, the truth, and the life" (John 14:6). We will rise again, and receive this gift from the Lord, as He is the resurrection, saying "I am the resurrection" (John 11:25). He is also the door, through which we enter into the highest blessing. What is the benefit of speaking about wisdom? "The Lord possessed me at the beginning of His way, before His works of old" (Proverbs 8:22), righteousness is the wisdom of the Lord, with whom their feet are beautiful.

Origen repeats "God is not the God of the dead, but of the living" (Matthew 22:32). Who are "the dead"? They are the sinners, who do not possess the one who says: "I am the life" (John 11:25), whose works die (Hebrews 6:1). And we know who the living are, they are those who lead their lives with Christ and He remains with them.

---

184 *In Luc. hom. 18:4.*
185 *In Luc. hom. 19:4.*

13

ORIGEN AND THE HOLY SPIRIT

Origen dedicated a chapter in his article on "First Principles" to the Holy Spirit, including his views in response to Marcion and Valentinus, specifically mentioning that the one Holy Spirit inspired both the Old and New Covenants, just as there is the one Father and the one Son. In the Old Covenant, the Spirit worked through the prophets, and now after the coming of the Savior, it flows abundantly upon the entire Church, teaching how to read the Scriptures with a spiritual sense, and spreading the grace associated with the work of the Holy Spirit.

Origen affirmed that the Holy Spirit is not just a divine power or energy, but is a divine hypostasis. The apostles, after enumerating the gifts of the Spirit, declare that "all these are the work of the one and the same Spirit, and he distributes them to each one, just as he determines" (1 Cor 12:11). When we contemplate the phrases "as he determines," "works," and "distributes," we realize that it is an essence derived from the self, active. Origen uses words from the book of Acts to confirm this same idea, "For they had seen the Holy Spirit and us"

(Acts 28:15), "The Holy Spirit said" (2:13), "This is what the Holy Spirit says" (11:21). He acknowledges that the Spirit works in creation.

The Divinity of the Holy Spirit

Origen affirmed the divinity of the Holy Spirit, as the Spirit is in essence in the Law as in the Gospel. He is always with the Father and the Son, and like the Father and the Son, existing always and forever. The divinity of Christ is clear, not only in the miracles he performed and the prophecies he fulfilled, but also in the power by which he works in believers. Christians still retain the works of the Holy Spirit who appeared in the form of a dove. They cast out evil spirits, perform healing miracles, and prophesy specific events, according to the will of the Logos... We should not assume that the Spirit knows God as we know Him, through revelation from the Son. Because if the Holy Spirit knew the Father in this way, it would mean that he transitioned from a state of ignorance to a state of knowledge. And it is certainly foolish to attribute ignorance to him, if we dare to say that there was a time when the Holy Spirit did not exist, and did not know the Father. He is mentioned after the Father and the Son, because through him the work is completed, and because in the life of holiness, perfection only comes at the end.

The Work of the Holy Spirit

I believe that the grace of the Holy Spirit grants all kinds of talents. Some are given words of wisdom, others words of knowledge, and others faith, and so on for each individual who is able to accept it. The work of the Father and the work of the Son spread without distinction to anyone in all creation, but only the saints alone possess a share in the Holy Spirit. Based on this, it is said, "No one can say Jesus is Lord except by the Holy Spirit" (1 Cor 3:12). Even the apostles themselves are not considered worthy in the end to hear his word except barely, "You will receive power when the Holy Spirit comes upon you" (Acts

8:1). It logically follows - in my opinion - that "whoever speaks a word against the Son of Man, it shall be forgiven him," because whoever has a share in the word and logic, if he stops living according to this logic, he will fall into ignorance, and may qualify for forgiveness. But whoever was counted as deserving to partake in the Holy Spirit and then turned away, by this act denies the Holy Spirit. The distinguished grace of the work of the Holy Spirit must be deserved, and those who receive it must (for example) be:

A. Thirsty for the Lord, longing for the Holy Spirit to grant them divine talents. The apostle says, "I long to see you so that I may impart to you some spiritual gift" (Rom 11:1).

B. Those who deserve it through faith in Christ, for the grace of the Holy Spirit is given to believers.

C. Those purified by the law, who work by the commandments of the Lord and carry them out. And you who desire the holy anointing to acquire the grace of the Holy Spirit, you must submit to the purification of the law, listen to the word of the Lord, cut off your internal sins, cast off your barbaric habits, and become humble enough to receive the grace of the Spirit.

D. The humble and meek, pure of heart, whose lives are praised for their virtues and love. "Not all who are of Israel are Israelites" (Rom 6:9). And not everyone who is baptized with water is therefore baptized with the Holy Spirit. Just as not everyone who is enrolled to receive religious principles after their baptism is outside the circle of the Spirit. For Cornelius, a centurion of the Italian cohort, was found worthy to receive the Holy Spirit even before coming to the water (Acts 44:10). While Simon, who had previously received baptism, was deprived of the Holy Spirit, due to his lack of sincerity in seeking this grace (Acts 8:13-25).

We read that the Holy Spirit does not dwell on all people indiscriminately, but on the holy and blessed ones among them. The Spirit of God dwells in the "pure in heart" (Matthew 8:5), those who have *purified themselves from sin. Just as it does not dwell in a body that has surrendered to sin, even if it had dwelt in it in the past. The Holy Spirit does not tolerate sharing and companionship with an evil spirit. There is no doubt that when we commit a sin, an evil spirit comes and dwells in our hearts. The apostle says, "Do not grieve the Holy Spirit of God, with whom you were sealed for the day of redemption" (Ephesians 4:30), and our holy deeds prepare a place for Him to rest. In every generation, the wisdom of God enters the holy souls and transforms them into friends of the Lord. The Holy Spirit comes to the pure who possess faith and love and stay away from the wicked.*

2. We need the Holy Spirit to grant us unity with the Father through the Son. Our Lord Jesus is the only way that leads us to this unity. He offered His holy blood as the price for it, and unity was realized through the Holy Spirit. It is impossible for us to be in communion with the Father or the Son without communion with the Holy Spirit.

3. We need the Holy Spirit to dwell in us, to show us that "God is love" (1 John 4:8). Not through mere words and theoretical ideas, but by the presence of "love" itself within us. The Holy Spirit, proceeding from the Father, who is the "Spirit of truth, who proceeds from the Father" (John 15:26), searches for the deserving soul capable of accepting His great love, the love of God, which He desires to show to it.

4. The Holy Spirit has a role in our prayers. If we acknowledge our shortcomings, it leads us to what is above the heavens. Wherever a (Christian) prays, they do not stop at the gates of heaven, but enter under the guidance of the Spirit of God.

5. The Holy Spirit gives us the word of God and divine knowledge. "The Spirit searches all things, even the deep things of God" (1 Corinthians 2:10), as no human soul can search "all things". The Holy Spirit reveals the mystery of the Holy Trinity.

6. The Holy Spirit helps us to be witnesses to the Gospel and teach others the truth.

Spiritual understanding of the Holy Scriptures is a grace from the Holy Spirit, granted to believers so that they may enter the eternal wedding between the Lord Jesus Christ and themselves, and enjoy divine wisdom and its mysteries. It gives knowledge and wisdom. Origen took this idea from his teacher, the saint Clemens, who decided that understanding the Scriptures is not for everyone, but for the Gnostics who are guided by the Holy Spirit, who gives knowledge. "We pray that the light that comes through 'knowing the glory of God in our hearts' (2 Cor 6:4) enables us to conceive and understand the things of God" because "all who are led by the Spirit of God are sons of God" (Rom 14:8).

The Holy Spirit, who is the Spirit of Christ, descended upon Him in His baptism on our behalf, so that He may dwell within us and grant us adoption to the Father. The Lord asks us to call God "Our Father who art in heaven." Saint Paul says, "For you did not receive the spirit of slavery to fall back into fear, but you have received the spirit of adoption as sons, by whom we cry, 'Abba! Father!' The Spirit himself bears witness with our spirit that we are children of God" (Rom 15:8-17). As John the Evangelist says, "But to all who did receive Him, who believed in His name, He gave the right to become children of God" (John 12:1).

The Holy Spirit in the Old Covenant

Some of the Jewish prophets were intelligent before accepting the gift of prophecy and divine inspiration, and some became intelligent through the intellectual enlightenment that was the gift of prophecy. These were chosen by divine providence to be entrusted with the Holy Spirit based on the delicate freedom of their lives, through which they faced danger even unto death without fear. Through baptism, the inner man is created, and our nature is renewed by the Holy Spirit, so that we may live as children of the Lord and take on the new life in Christ. The Holy Spirit renews the face of the earth, through the grace of the

Spirit, nullifying the deeds of the old man (Col 3:9), and beginning to walk in the new life (Rom 6:4).

Enjoying the Spirit of Sanctification.

The Father gave existence to all creation, and the Son gives intellect and word to all capable, and the Holy Spirit deals with the lives of believers. Saint Clement of Alexandria says: "The divine teacher created man from dust, renewed him with water, and nurtured him with the Spirit." What does the saint mean by that? The divine teacher Jesus Christ and his Spirit are used in the Church, not only to give us sonship to the Lord, to always nurture us with divine life, but also to grant us sanctification in Christ Jesus, meaning the believer becomes holy as the Lord is holy (Leviticus 11:44-45). In the Old Testament, man felt sanctification as a burden that could not be borne, and now that the Lord gives us his Holy Spirit to dwell in us, sanctification has become delightful that the children of the Lord enjoy. He becomes the natural life of the spiritual man, where the Holy Spirit purifies the soul, mind, heart, senses, and all members of his body. He takes the gift of wisdom with the power of the Spirit in them, guiding them and teaching them perfection without ceasing. The Holy Spirit manifests his grace with power, and is called the "Spirit of Sanctification".

The Holy Spirit and Victory

Through prayer, the Church implores the Lord, expressing her love for him. The Lord promised his disciples to send them his Holy Spirit, who alone has the power to elevate our minds and enlighten our souls so that we may enjoy the relationship with the Father through his only Son. This is what Saint Paul means regarding the intercession of the Spirit for the saints according to the will of the Lord.

Origen says that prayer is the work of the Holy Trinity in our lives, for the Father shines light upon us, the Son teaches us, and the Holy Spirit sanctifies our frozen minds to become spiritual. David says: "To you I lift up my eyes, O you who are enthroned in the heavens" (Psalm 123:1), "To you, O Lord, I lift up my soul" (Psalm 25:1). How? The soul is lifted up to the highest and follows the Spirit until it clings to him. Truly, Saint Paul says: "Likewise the Spirit helps us in our weakness; for we do not know how to pray as we ought, but that very Spirit intercedes with sighs too deep for words" (Romans 8:26). And the Spirit cries out in the hearts of the blessed, knowing well our sighs, and knowing those who have fallen. He intercedes on our behalf, accepting our sighs for his great love and mercy upon us.

The Grace of the Spirit and the Glory of the Lord

It is easy for anyone to glorify the Lord with their mouth, but we need the grace of the Spirit that gives us inner joy, to glorify him with our minds, hearts, and senses. Through this divine grace, the believer enjoys heavenly life, which is a life filled with hymns and glorifying the Lord. By faith, we must worship the Lord, the Creator of all.

If someone deserves the company of the Holy Spirit through a mysterious knowledge that cannot be described, he will undoubtedly experience peace and joy in his heart, so that his soul cannot be disturbed or accept any feeling of regret. As for Paul and those like him, it is said that the Holy Spirit comforts them in the midst of tribulations, and we enjoy the great grace of the Lord in Jesus Christ, which is poured into our hearts through the Holy Spirit (Romans 5:5).

The Filling with the Holy Spirit

The gift of the grace of the Spirit is in the form of "oil" which is the transformation from sin to being filled with the Holy Spirit, through which we reconcile with the Father and become His children, through the Lord Jesus Christ Himself "to whom be glory and power forever. Amen." Human nature is weak and needs the power of the Holy Spirit. The person in whom the Spirit is strong triumphs.

14

INTRODUCTION TO CREATION

In the first set of articles by Origen (1-5), we realize his longing for the salvation (if possible) of all learners, whether philosophers or common people. The Church does not underestimate philosophers and does not want to engage in hostile dialogue with them. The door of divine salvation is open to all classes with the spirit of sincere love and the desire for all humanity to come together as one family of learners and common people, men and women, old and young, children, until the great day of the Lord comes when everyone will be filled with joy and appreciation, and true believers will carry the icon of the Holy Trinity, the lover of all humanity.

In the second set of articles (6-10), everyone looks forward through the love, care, and divine grace of God, so that every believer considers what all classes receive as if he himself has received it, so that no one envies his brother, mocks another, or seeks isolation from the rest of humanity.

In the third set of articles (11-13), all believers taste the fatherhood of the Father, which those who have become like Him are not deprived of, but they praise the incarnate Word of God for the salvation of every member, and everyone experiences the work of the Holy Spirit, who takes from the Son and bestows it on the believers with His amazing love.

And now in the fourth set of articles (14-16) concerning the creation of the universe and the role of angels in the lives of believers, and the stance of Satan and his evil angels. Satan and his angels seek to deceive the people of God so that they do not attain the heavenly inheritance that they lost by hating the divine truth. The discussion here is about the creation of the universe, the work of the angels, and the resistance of Satan, with the aim of humanity tasting the wonderful divine love. The goal of this fourth set is to ignite the hearts of believers, if possible, with the fires of God's supreme love, and to draw their hearts to touch the heavenly glories.

What benefit do you gain as a believer from knowing the creation of the universe, the exalted status of the angels, and the downfall of the demons?

Firstly: What is mentioned here about the creation of the universe reveals the love of the Creator that cannot be expressed. Every believer sees that God works tirelessly so that each believer carries the image of God and everyone takes pride in God's love for His creation, as He calls us to the day of His final coming, so our souls rejoice and praise Him, saying, "Come, Lord Jesus!" (Rev 22:20).

Secondly: Regarding his discussion about the angels, Origen provided us with a practical testimony that a believer can taste, causing his heart to ignite with heavenly love, and realizing that the angels accompany us in our gatherings with each other, and delight in the work of the Holy Trinity within us.

Thirdly: Origen emphasized that the angels delight in the work of the Savior on our behalf, desiring to serve us with wonderful joy in all stages of our lives, and that the nature of the heavenly beings is serving spirits for those who believe in Him for eternal life (1 Tim 1:16).

Fourthly: The angels desire to serve the believers, who presented the word of God their lives on earth for them until the day they depart from the world. The work of the angels does not stop at this point, but their relationship with us increases even when our souls depart from the body.

Fifthly: Origen presented the holy jealousy of the angels and their ceaseless movements to serve the believers, never ceasing in their work for their salvation, the salvation of their brethren, and even the salvation of their enemies and those who resist them.

Sixthly: Origen elaborated on their work for our salvation while speaking briefly when discussing the work of Satan and his evil angels against us, for God does not want us to be preoccupied with evil spirits and their resistance to us, but with the spirit of hope we crush the forces of darkness.

Seventhly: What concerns the Lord is not that we focus on defeating Satan and his angels, but that we live a life filled with the Lord without losing our spiritual happiness and the praise of our souls.

Eighth: Origen's sayings about the abundance of angels longing to serve humans, especially believers, in every small and big thing, make us truly filled with hope that we live in our exile on earth as if in heaven, and we realize that we enjoy a foretaste of heaven so we do not fear death, but rather we rejoice as we eagerly race towards heaven. Believers feel jubilant when one of their loved ones passes on to heaven. We do not feel distressed here in the world, but rather we are jubilant on earth and our jubilation increases as time passes, so we feel that heaven is not far from us, because our hearts have become the kingdom of God.

15

ORIGEN AND CREATION

Why did Origen focus on talking about the creation of the universe?

Philosophers often discussed the creation of the universe, as did simple believers, as the Bible begins by saying: "In the beginning God created the heavens and the earth" (Genesis 1:2). Both philosophers and simple believers had their questions about the creation of the universe. Origen dealt with the science of creation philosophically to educate learners and correct some of the mistakes of philosophers, while at the same time wanting to provide an explanation of the Creator's purpose in a simple scriptural manner.

Gerald Bostock believes that Origen's philosophical framework for the creation of the universe was clarified in his interpretation of Genesis 1:6. "And God said, 'Let there be a vault between the waters to separate water from water.' So God made the vault and separated the water under the vault from the water above it. And it was so. God called the vault 'sky'." Origen says: When the believer is connected to the upper waters that are above in the heavens, they become heavenly and seek higher spiritual matters, not earthly thoughts, but heavenly ones. They seek what is above where Christ is seated at the right hand of God (Colossians 3:1), deserving to enjoy God's praise, "God saw that it was good."[1]

Did God need time in creation?

The Lord who created the whole world did not need time to create the heavens and the earth, because if things were created in six days, we must understand the meaning of "six days." Origen says that days did not exist before the creation of the sun, moon, and planets. It is clear that the days mentioned in the first chapter of the book of Genesis were not intended to be a literal succession of days.

How was human nature created?

Origen was happy to confirm that the nature of the body was created from nothing after a period of time, and came into existence from non-existence. The material body remains, but for a certain time. Just as it did not exist before it was created, and it will dissolve into non-existence. This philosophical suggestion connects Origen with what is mentioned in the Gospel that heaven and earth will pass away (Matt 5:18), and that this world has a beginning and an end. And that man enters time with his birth and leaves it with his death.

Is there a connection between creation and salvation?

Origen believes that creation presents salvific purposes, so the soul can choose between good and evil. This choice requires that human nature be able to connect between these two systems. Man can know the hidden secrets of heaven through the things perceived in this world. God created everything with wisdom, so by creating visible things on

---

[1] *In Gen. Hom 1: 2.*

earth, we can understand the spiritual things that are invisible, and man becomes acquainted with the things in paradise.

What do we perceive from the harmony of the creative world?

Creation revealed that the Creator is the wonderful good Lord. He created the world with a creative harmony through His divine wisdom, supreme care, and concern for providing free will especially for rational beings. As man advances in knowledge, he realizes some amazing things in creation that were hidden from humanity in previous generations. Creation testifies to the goodness, justice, mercy, and care of God, and confirms that things do not happen by chance but by divine decree.

Why did Origen focus his efforts on two problems: the origin of matter and the origin of knowledge of God?

Origen criticized the philosophers of his time, as they were characterized by ambiguity in discussing the origin of matter, and their lack of understanding of the knowledge of God because ambiguity misled them.

Did God create evil?

Origen believes that evil was not created, but it originates from within the human soul. Sin is the main cause of evil. Matter does not possess the power of rebellion, but actions filled with disturbances and annoyances are behind evil. By saying this, Origen confirms that evil comes from the inspiration of Satan and his evil angels and deviant humans.

Did creation materialize in a dry manner?

Origen understood what the Apostle Paul said: "What no eye has seen, what no ear has heard, and what no human mind has conceived— the things God has prepared for those who love him" (1 Corinthians 2:9). Origen described the Creator as eternal joy, full of love, and the source of wisdom. In all of this, humans cannot express the attributes of the Creator because He is not like humans. Here I remember what a college girl in America said to me in the seventies or eighties: "Will we live in eternity looking to God and praising Him endlessly, with no other work for us?" When she presented me with this question, I remembered what a believer in Russia wrote about eternal life, that if we asked a worm, "What do you think of the human mind?" It does not comprehend human life and their capabilities. The difference is that we often think we are capable of explaining divine thought and companionship with Him, and we imagine eternal life, endless in a human way!

Will there be another earthly world after the end of this world, then a third world, and a fourth world?

Origen rejected this idea that prevailed among some philosophers, saying that he did not know what evidence they relied on to prove this theory. He rejected the prevailing ideas that after a person's death, they return to the world, die again, and this process is repeated several times.

Is it fitting for a believer to hate the world?

The scholar Origen says that the wicked person hates all creatures, while the good person filled with love is served by creatures. Saint Basil the Great emphasized strongly, especially in his final sermons, how a believer can learn from the inert nature, fish, insects, and even predatory animals what is essential for his building. The good person passes through his life as the children of Israel passed through the Red Sea, while the Egyptians who resisted God drowned in it. God promised us in the book of Isaiah: "But now, this is what the Lord says— he who created you, Jacob, he who formed you, Israel: 'Do not fear, for I have redeemed you; I have summoned you by name; you are mine. When you pass through the waters, I will be with you; and when you pass through the rivers, they will not sweep over you. When you walk through the fire, you will not be burned; the flames will not set you ablaze.'" (Isaiah 43:1-2).

Origen says: The good person does not fear anything, because creation serves him (Psalm 8:6-9).

16

ORIGEN AND THE ANGELS[2]

In the introduction to his book "De Principiis," Origen explained the Church's teaching about angels and demons. It is stated in its tradition that angels are the servants of God and therefore His creation; as for the time of their creation and the nature of their existence, it left it for inquiry.[3]

What does the Bible say about the will of angels?

Origen says: ["Bless the Lord, you His angels, who excel in strength, who do His word, heeding the voice of His word" (Psalm 103:20) in carrying out the will of God, and in striving to destroy the wicked, there is evidence that the angels stand before God and serve Him as if they were His right hand (Luke 19:1), due to their good will.][4]

---

2   Cf. Jean Daniélou: *The Angels and their Mission According to the Fathers of the Church*, translated by David Heimann, 1933.
3   Jaroslav Pelikan: *The Christian Tradition, 1. The Emergence of the Catholic Tradition (100-600)*, Chicago, 1971, p. 134-5.
4   De Principiis 1:8 (Henri De Lubac).

Are the wills of rational beings free?

Origen affirms the free will of angels, demons, and humans and their ability to do good and evil, and also believes that God alone is holy by nature. He says: [Our conviction is that among rational beings there is none who is incapable of practicing good and evil. But this does not necessarily mean that there is no rational being who cannot practice evil, confirming that all have practiced evil. This is like saying that every person has the ability to become a sailor, but it does not necessarily mean that everyone becomes sailors. Or if we say that every person has the ability to learn a language and its rules or to study medicine, this is not evidence that all humans are either teachers or doctors. By this logic, if we say that there is no one who cannot resist evil, this does not mean that every rational creature has done so. On the other hand, saying that there is no one who cannot do good does not confirm that every rational creature has practiced it. We see that the devil himself is capable of doing good. But this fact did not lead him to desire good, or to make a serious attempt to acquire virtues. We have learned from passages taken from the prophets that he was righteous at some point. When he was residing in God's paradise among the cherubim. So he had the ability to do good or evil. If it happened that he turned away from good, he had completely turned his mind towards evil. The same applies to other creatures, they have the ability to choose between this and that, if they exercise their free will, and flee from evil while being attached to good. As for the nature of the Holy Spirit, it does not engage in defilement, as He is holy by nature... There is a category of rational creatures who have surrendered to evil to the extent that they have lost the desire or even the ability to return to good, as their evil deeds have turned into delight and joy.][5]

---

5   *De Principiis 1:8 (Henri De Lubac).*

Do angels have a role in the church?

Origen sees that every person is served by a good angel and another evil one (the devil). Origen says: "The angel of the Lord encamps around those who fear him and delivers them" (Psalm 34:7). This means that if a group of people gather to glorify Christ, each one of them will have their accompanying angel, if they all fear the Lord. Each angel will be in the company of those assigned to guard and guide them. So when the saints gather, there are two churches, one of people and the other of angels.[6]

What is the role of angels with the people of God in the Old Testament?

A. The angels, as friends of the bridegroom, guide the church, the people of God, during its betrothal period, that is, in the Old Testament. But the church longs for the kiss of the bridegroom himself, that is, for his coming to her in person.

- ❖ (The church says) When I was preparing myself for marriage to the son of the king, the firstborn of all creation, the angels accompanied me and served me, bringing me the law as a wedding gift. It is said that the law was announced through the angels by a mediator (Galatians 3:19). And as the world approached its end, and (the bridegroom) did not grace me with his presence, I see only his servants ascending and descending around me. Therefore, I poured out my prayers before you, O (Father) Father of my bridegroom, pleading that you have mercy on my love and send him to me so that he does not need to speak to me through his angelic servants, but comes to me in person.[7]

---

6   *On Prayer 31:4.*
7   *Comm. on Song of Songs 1.*

- ❖ The entire Jewish worship was a simulation of gold. While if one turned to the Lord, and the veil was removed from before him, he would see the true gold.[8]

- ❖ The role of angels was limited to beginnings or arrangements until the Lord Christ (the bridegroom) came. This concept encompasses the entire theological thought related to the tasks of angels, in a general framework.

B. The announcement of the law was the main gift that God gave to his people, through the service of the angels.

C. According to what is mentioned in the Book of Wisdom, the people throughout their journey of exodus were not only served by the angels, but they also fed on the food of the angels. God gave them bread from heaven, prepared without effort, containing everything delicious and sweet in taste (Wisdom 16:20). Origen demands going out and embarking on a spiritual journey through the wilderness of this life, so that we may obtain the bread of the angels.

- ❖ Do not be disturbed by the loneliness of the wilderness, for you will not receive the manna from heaven and feed on the bread of the angels unless you dwell in his tents.[9]

Dr. Origen tells us that the Ark of the Covenant, its golden cover, and the cherubim, even the temple itself, were all given to Israel by the angels.[10]

---

8   *Comm. on Song of Songs 2.*
9   *In Num. hom. 17:3.*
10 *Cf. Comm. on Song of Songs 2.*

What is the role of angels in the service of the New Covenant?

Origen sees one of these angels appearing in the person of the Macedonian who sought help from Saint Paul.[11]

The role of angels in the churches began with their service to souls that were still steeped in paganism.

- ❖ The angels assisted the apostles in carrying out their ministry of preaching and completing their evangelistic work.[12]

Did the angels serve the nations?

Origen, like his teacher Saint Clement of Alexandria, believed that the governing angelic forces were distributed among nations and cities,[13] saying: "[Spiritual forces were assigned to oversee the affairs of specific nations in this world.]"[14]

Origen attributes to the angels a role in the origin of different languages, similar to the Jewish tradition, but their spiritual service was primary.[15]

- ❖ It is mentioned in the Bible that there are rulers for each nation. For example, in the Book of Daniel, there is mention of a prince of Persia and another of Greece, who, as the sensory meaning of the words indicates, are not human but of the forces. Similarly, in the Book of Ezekiel, there is mention of a king of Tyre, clearly a specific spiritual force.[16]

---

11   *In Luc. hom. 12.*
12   *Hom. in Num., 11, 4.*
13   *Stromata 6:17.*
14   *De Principiis 3:3:3.*
15   *Contra Celsus 5:30.*
16   *De Principiis 3:3 (Henri De Lubac).*

The angels assigned to the nations were unable to stop the flood of wickedness in them. "[Before the birth of Christ, they were of little benefit to those they were assigned to, and their attempts were unsuccessful. What did the angels do for the Egyptians they were assigned to help? There was not a single guided one who believed in God."].[17]

What was the service of the angels at the birth of Christ?

Origen says: "[The coming of Christ into the world was a great joy for those entrusted with the care of people and nations."]. Origen explained the jealousy of the angels to descend with the Word.[18]

> ❖ When the angels saw the Prince of Heaven walking on earth, they entered through the path he opened, following their Lord's footsteps, obedient to his will, as he entrusted them with the care of those who believed in him. So the angels are indeed in service to your salvation... as if I hear them saying among themselves: "If (the Lord) has taken on flesh to suffer, how can we remain idle? Come, angels, let us all descend from heaven." This is why there was a multitude of heavenly forces praising and glorifying God at the birth of Christ. The place was filled with them.[19]

Origen explains that the shepherds of Bethlehem are allegorically like the angels of the nations. "The shepherds can be considered like the angels who are entrusted with the people. They all needed help, so they could rule over these nations that are under their authority. And to them the angel came to announce the birth of the true shepherd.[20]

---

17 *In Luc. hom. 12.*
18 *In Luc. hom. 12.*
19 *In Ex. hom. 1:7.*
20 *In Luc. hom. 12.*

What is the service of the angels at the ascension of Christ?

The entry of the incarnate Word into heaven seems like a previous announcement directed to the heavenly forces. With Origen, we look at Isaiah 63: 1-3, and the reference to the blood of the sufferings of Christ.

- ❖ When the victorious one presented his risen body from death, the concerned forces said: "Who is coming with red garments from Bozrah?" As for those who were with him, they cried out to those standing at the gates of heaven: "Open up, O eternal gates, that the King of glory may enter (Psalm 24:7)."[21]

What is the service of the angels in the final coming?

- ❖ When the Son of Man comes in the glory of his Father .. the angels will be with him, preserving their ranks of glory when "the Word" comes in this way with his angels, he will enjoy some of his glory and the radiance of his angels, each according to his deeds.[22]

What is the service of the angels in proclaiming?

- ❖ The role of the angels is not limited to just crediting them with small tasks for the sake of the Gospel, but the flying angels in the midst of heaven (Rev 6:14) while performing their duties proclaim the Gospel to all nations.[23]

- ❖ If among the people there are those who have been honored with the message of evangelism, and if Christ Himself brings the good news and preaches the Gospel to the poor, then certainly

---

21 *Comm. in Jo.,* 6,56.v
22 *Comm. on Matt. 12:30 (ANF).*
23 *Comm. on John 1:14.*

His servants, who are His angels, will not be exempt from also being eager to evangelize. Therefore, the angel came to the shepherds, and with him "the glory of the Lord shone around them," and said to them: "Do not be afraid, for behold, I bring you good tidings of great joy which will be to all people. For there is born to you this day in the city of David a Savior, who is Christ the Lord" (Luke 2:10-11). At a time when people did not have knowledge of the mystery of the Gospel, those who are the greatest inhabitants of the heavens, the army of God, praised the Lord saying: "Glory to God in the highest, and on earth peace, goodwill toward men." And as they praised Him, they returned to heaven, leaving us to contemplate how the joy brought by the birth of Christ is glory to God in the highest. They humbled themselves on earth, then returned to their place of rest, to glorify God in the highest through Jesus Christ. The angels also marvel at the peace that comes with the birth of Christ on earth, the cradle of wars, into which Satan fell, the morning star from heaven, to enter into war with Jesus and be defeated.[24]

What is the service of angels in the sacred mysteries?

Origen sees angels as servants, with their role in the church's work. For example, in baptism, the angel receives with joy the one who receives baptism for the divine blessings he receives. The matter does not stop at attendance and joy, but Origen sees in the angel a physician, with a role in preparing the person for baptism. He also has a role in the baptism itself as one who serves the mystery. Angels are also present in every Christian gathering.

❖ Come, O king, to receive the one who has turned away from his original sin, turned away from the devil's creed. Receive him as

---

24 *Comm. on John 1:13 (ANF)*.

a thorough physician. Give him warmth and healing. Receive him, and give him the baptism of the second birth.[25]

❖ At the time when we received the mystery of faith, there were heavenly forces around you receiving you, a priestly service of angels, the church of the firstborn (Hebrews 12:23). If we understand that the word "Israel" means "seeing the Lord in the mind," we will see that this name becomes more fitting when used for the angels who serve us. Just as the Lord said about children, and you were a child at your baptism, "Their angels in heaven always see the face of My Father who is in heaven" (Matthew 10:18). Thus the children of "Israel" see the face of the Lord and are present and give you the secrets of faith.[26]

❖ If the angels of the Lord are present around those who fear Him, and will save them, and if what Jacob says is true, not only in relation to him, but also in relation to all those who are dedicated to God - full of knowledge - when he speaks of the angels who deliver us from all evil, then when a number of people gather for the glory of Jesus, an angel stands around each one who fears the Lord, standing next to the one entrusted with his protection and guidance. So, when the saints come together, there is a double church, one of people, and the other of angels.[27]

❖ With the spirit of the Holy Scriptures, the angels rejoice and pray with us. And since the angels are present in the church, where they deserve to be, it is the duty of praying women to have something covering their heads "because of the angels". The angels assist the saints and rejoice in the church. Truly, we cannot see them with our sin-blinded eyes, but the disciples of Jesus saw them as He promised them: "Most assuredly, I say to

---

25   *In Eze. hom. 1:7.*
26   *In Jos. hom. 9:4.*
27   Origen, *De or., 31,5 (ACW 19).*

you, hereafter you shall see heaven open, and the angels of God ascending and descending upon the Son of Man" (John 1:51).[28]

❖ Referring to the words "when you became a child through the font in Christ," it can be said that there are no holy angels with those who are in sin. During their period of rebellion, they come under the leadership of the angels of Satan. But after their renewal, they are entrusted to a holy angel by the one who redeemed them with His blood, and because of their purity, they behold the face of God.[29]

What is the service of the angels to the Lord Christ?

❖ The angels of God came to Jesus to serve Him (Matthew 11:4), and we should not believe that their service to Jesus was only for a short time, during His incarnation among people, and while He was in the midst of those who believed in Him, where He came not to be served, but to serve (Luke 27:22). How many angels, in your belief, will come to serve Him when He decides to gather the children of Israel one by one, gather them from the dispersion, call them to Him, and deliver them from fear? (Isaiah 12:27; John 16:10; 52:11; Acts 21:2). Do they not contribute more than the apostles to the growth of the church, to the point where John in the Revelation says that appointed angels are set over the churches (Revelation 20:1)? It was not in vain that the angels of God ascended and descended upon the Son of Man, and they were seen by those whose eyes were enlightened by the light of knowledge (John 51:1).[30]

❖ At all times, each angel looks at the face of God the Father, even the angels of the little ones in the church (Matthew 10:18), and

---

28 *Hom. in Luc., 23.*
29 *Comm. on Matt. 13: 28 (ANF).*
30 *On Prayer 11:3 (ACW).*

beholds the Creator. They pray with us and cooperate with us as much as possible in what we chant.[31]

❖ Since Allah knows the free will of every human being, and He has foreseen what each person will do, He has carefully arranged for each one an angel suitable for him according to his merit, giving him so that he may pray for him. Allah says to those who possess these qualities or those, that He has sent to them a guardian angel who works with them for their salvation, starting from a certain time and remaining with them until another time. And He says about another angel: "I will send another angel, perhaps of a higher rank, in proportion to his superiority over the one before him." And for another person who dedicated themselves to noble education, but then succumbed to weakness and returned to material matters, I will strip him of the assistance of the forces, which, upon his departure from him - according to his merit - a certain evil force will seize him and find the opportunity to benefit from his weakness, thus luring him, if he shows readiness for sin, to commit this vice or that.[32]

Who are the guardian angels?

The teaching about the guardian angels was not new to Origen, as it had already been mentioned in the writings of the so-called Barnabas[33] and the Shepherd of Hermas,[34] and in the works of Saint Clement of Alexandria,[35] and had a basis in the Bible (Genesis 16:48). This teaching appears in early Christian writings, and Origen developed it to a great extent.

---

31 *On Prayer 11:5.*
32 *On Prayer 6:4 (ACW).*
33 *Pseudo-Barn.*, 18,1.
34 *Vis.*, 5, 1-4.
35 *Ecl.*, 41, 48.

❖ We must say that the human soul is under the supervision of an angel, acting as a parent for it.[36]

The fathers of the fourth century embraced this same belief. For Saint Basil, an angel is assigned to each believer; this is if we do not drive him away from us by sin. He guards the soul like an army.[37]

❖ When a person accepts faith, Christ, who redeemed him with his blood from the evil one, entrusts him to a holy angel who, because of his purity, beholds the face of God the Father.[38]

❖ So that evil spirits may not find a place in the human soul later on, the wisdom and care of God saw fit to provide young children, and those who are nothing but infants in Christ, and unable to defend themselves against the deception of the devil and the attacks of evil spirits, with angels and guardian heroes, appointed by Him as their guides and educators (1 Corinthians 1:3; Galatians 2:4).[39]

Origen believes that angels guide nations and churches, in addition to their role as guardians of individuals. The higher ranks of angels are assigned more important tasks. In his sermons in Caesarea, Origen says that angels of the highest ranks are assigned to individuals of higher intellectual stature, and therefore of greater responsibility than those assigned to the general public. If some of them fall from their deserved level, they are stripped of their heavenly guardians and entrusted to angels of a lower rank.[40]

Angels, demons, and humans were created equal. The difference

---

36   *Comm. in Matt., 13,5.*
37   *Hom. in Ps. 33:6. See also Gregory of Nyssa, Hom. Cant., 7; Hilary, Tract. Ps. 124; Tract. Ps. 137: "All the faithful are aided by the services of these divine ministers according to what has been written: "The angel of the Lord surrounds those who fear Him' (Psalm 33:8)": Eusebius, Praep. Ev., 13; Gregory the Wonder-worker, Pan. Orig., PG 10, 1061 BC.*
38   *Comm. in Matt., 13, 28.*
39   *Comm. on the Songs of Songs, book 2:3 (ACW).*
40   *Joseph Wilson Trigg: Origen, SCM Press Ltd, 1983, p.105.*

even among celestial beings is a result of their behavior based on their free will.

Before guidance, humans were slaves to the devil, but afterwards they have a special angel to encourage them to do good deeds and protect them from evil angels. Also, angels of believers are with them in an unseen church.

The sense of satanic influence was strong, as Origen dedicated a chapter in his book "First Principles" to discuss how to combat the devil and opposing forces against the human race as mentioned in the Bible. However, he puts a lot of effort into putting the devil's role in its proper place. Origen says that some simple Christians believe that the devil's power is what drives humans towards evil. And if there were no demons, there would be no sin, which is not true. Sin comes from within. But demons seize the opportunity of our fall to make our situation worse. However, they actually implant evil thoughts in our hearts. In any case, we are not alone against evil forces, as there are good spirits that help us. Here Origen mentions a paragraph from the second century in the Shepherd of Hermas[41] talking about the existence of two angels for each person, one for good and the other for evil, competing for the person.[42]

❖ As the Lord testifies in the Gospel that the hearts of sinners are surrounded by "seven demons" (Luke 26:11), we find the priest appropriately anointing with oil seven times before the Lord to expel the seven evil spirits from the person seeking purification.[43]

Origen applies what is mentioned in Psalm 91 to Christians, "For he will command his angels concerning you to guard you in all your ways" (Psalm 91:11), and comments: [The upright are those who need the help

---

41 *Mand 6:2:1-10.*
42 *De Principiis 3:2:4; Boniface Ramsey: Beginning to Read the Fathers, Paulist Press, 1985, p. 65-6.*
43 *In Lev. hom. 8:14 (G.W. Barkley - Frs. of the Church).*

of God's angels, so that the devil does not cause them to fall, and so that no arrow flying in the dark penetrates their hearts.].[44]

Origen assigns a role to the angels in the process of redemption. When he refers to the parable of the Good Samaritan regarding the repentance of the sinner, he writes: "As he was about to depart in the morning, he took two denarii from his money and gave them to the innkeeper, who undoubtedly symbolizes the angels of the church, instructing him to take care of the sick man and nurse him until he recovers."[45] In another passage, comparing the raising of Lazarus and the raising of the sinner, Origen notes that the body of Lazarus, after coming out of the tomb, was still wrapped in grave clothes. "One might wonder to whom the Lord directed his word 'unbind him.' It is not recorded that it was directed to the disciples, nor to the crowd, nor to those who were with Mary. Therefore, the words stating: 'The angels came and ministered to him,' in addition to the symbolic nature of the paragraph, do not allow us to assume that they were directed to anyone other than these."[46]

Origen distinguishes between praying in the presence of angels in general, and the specific presence of the guardian angel. "In the same way, we must believe that the angels, who are servants of God and guardians appointed by Him, are present with the person who prays, until they join him. The truth is that the angel assigned to each of us, even to the children in the church, who always behold the face of the Father, and witness the divinity of the Creator, prays with us and supports us as much as possible in what we ask for."[47]

This contribution of the guardian angel in our prayers, and their union with us in our supplications, is frequently mentioned in the writings of Origen. A Christian should not fear the devil, because "the

---

44   *Hom. in Num.*, 5, 3.
45   *Hom. in Luc.*, 34.
46   *Comm. in Jo.*, 28, 8.
47   *De or.*, 11,5 (ACW 19).

angel of the Lord encamps around those who fear God and delivers them. And because his angel who always beholds the face of the Father in heaven, raises his prayer along with the high priest to the God of all. He truly shares with those entrusted to his care in their prayers."[48]

The angels, therefore, move between the soul and heaven. "We truly believe that they ascend carrying the prayers of the people, then descend with each one, bringing with them whatever good things he desires, appointed by the Lord to present them to those they love."[49]

- ❖ Each of us is influenced by two angels: one for good and another for evil. If there is a good thought in our minds, there is no doubt that it is the angel of the Lord speaking to us. But if evil things come into our hearts, it is the angel of evil who addresses us.[50]

What is the role of angels in spiritual life?

The angelic assistance that comes to the soul at baptism continues throughout life's journey. Nothing will stop it except sins, which only sadden the angel of the soul.[51] Origen wrote: "There must be angels responsible for sacred matters, teaching concepts of eternal light, and divine knowledge."[52] He says: "Do not be afraid of loneliness in the wilderness, for the angels will soon come to accompany you." Origen was the first to affirm this characteristic in the work of angels and their concern for the beginnings of spiritual life. "See for yourself how they surround all the little ones who are overcome by fear. As for those who are more advanced, the angel of the Lord says to each of them: "I am with you in times of trial." As our perfection diminishes, we need an

---

48 *Contra Cels.*, 8,36.
49 *Ibid.*, 5, 4. See also *Hom. in Num.*, 11,5; *Hom'. in Lev.*, 9,8. Hilary has this testimony to give: "There is positive grounds to the teaching (auctoritas absoluta) that the angels preside over the prayers of the faithful. They offer to God every day the prayers of those who have been saved" (*Comm. in Matt.*, 18,5). See also *Tract. Ps. 129*.
50 *Ibid.*, 12.
51 Origen, *Hom. in Luc.*, 35.
52 *Hom. in Num.*, 14, 2.

angel to deliver us from evil. After we mature and surpass the stage where we are under the guidance of teachers and guides, we come under the leadership of Christ himself."[53] Here Origen confirms a general aspect of the doctrine related to angels, namely their relationship with the beginnings and preparations for spiritual life. The angels were among those who prepared the way for Christ in the Old Testament. They are the friends of the bridegroom who complete their joy by hearing his voice, after which they leave him with his bride.[54]

Angels - as the Gospel tells us - have a special relationship with children. Therefore, their role remains linked to the beginnings in spiritual life. They attract the soul to goodness with noble inspirations, as they instill fear of sin in it. By doing so, they prepare it to lack the word, and then withdraw from it. In its spiritual ascent, the soul first passes through the angelic realm, then surpasses it to reach the kingdom of God. The task of the angels is to guide the soul to the angelic realm, and then they disappear from before it.

Do the angels rejoice in our victory?

If you engage in battle, say with Paul: "We have become a spectacle to the world, to angels and to men" (1 Cor 9:4). For the whole world, and all the angels from the right and from the left, and all people, including those who are on God's side (Cor 12:1), and all others will listen to us as we struggle for our Christianity. Either the angels of heaven will rejoice in us, the rivers will clap their hands, the mountains will rejoice, and all the trees of the valley will clap their branches" (Psalm 8:98), or God will not allow the wicked joy to flood the underworld in celebration of our downfall.[55]

---

53 *Hom. in Num., 17, 4; E. Bettencourt, Doctrina ascetica Origenis, pp. 30 f.*
54 *Comm. in Matt., 12, 26. See also Comm. in Jo., 1, 25; Hom. in Num., 11, 3; 14, 3. See E. Bettencourt, op. cit., pp. 24-28.*
55 *Exhortation to Martyrdom, 18 (ACW).*

What is the position of the angels at the moment of our death?

The angels, as servants of the Savior, desire to work to assist us in our salvation. They help in the ascent of the souls of true believers, especially the martyrs, praising them: "Who is this!" "Quis est iste?". Origen portrays the angels in their support with great admiration for the martyrdom of the martyrs, as they did during the time of Christ's martyrdom.[56]

- ❖ A great crowd will gather to watch you as you fight, called to martyrdom.

- ❖ Who can follow the soul of the martyr in its ascent passing through the forces of the air, that is, the forces of the demons, taking its path towards the heavenly altar?! Blessed is that soul, which with its flowing crimson blood at its martyrdom brought defeat and humiliation to the ranks of the advanced demons of the air coming towards it. Blessed is the one whom the angels will sing as he enters heaven according to the prophetic words: "Who is this coming from Bozrah?"[57]

- ❖ When our body dissolves, and we begin to enter the holy places, in our crossing to the promised land, those who are truly holy, and their place in the holy of holies, see the angels surrounding them on their way, and when they reach the divine dwelling place, they stop to be carried on the shoulders by the angels, and lifted by their hands. This is all seen by the prophet in the spirit, when he said: "He will command his angels concerning you to guard you in all your ways" (Psalm 91:11). What is written in this psalm is undoubtedly closer and applicable to the upright than to the Lord. One can imagine the angels who bear

---

56   Origen, Hom. in Judic., 7,2.
57   *Ohm. in Judaic., 7,2. Gregory of Nyssa presents "the angels waiting on the death of martyrs in order to lead their souls into their abodes" (Serm. 40 Mart.).*

the responsibility of human souls, as they search for the good and bad deeds of the souls standing at the gates of heaven, by likening them to customs officers at the gates of cities.[58]

- ❖ At the end of the world, every angel will come forward for judgment and will take with them those who were entrusted to guide and assist them.[59]

- ❖ We must be cautious that if there is anything inappropriate in us, we may lose our place in the eyes of the bridegroom of our souls, or the angel assigned to us. If we do not take caution, we may receive a divorce decree. Either we will be deprived of our guardian angel, or we will be abandoned to another.[60]

What is the food of the angels?

- ❖ The angels also feed on the wisdom of God, and they receive strength to accomplish their tasks through their contemplation of truth and wisdom. We find it written in the Psalms that the angels also partake of food, sharing it with the people of God - the Hebrews - and thus becoming companions at the table. In relation to what is mentioned in that paragraph: "Man ate the bread of angels" (Psalm 25:78), we should not understand that the angels participate and feed forever on a specific type of material food, like that which was said to have descended upon those who came out of Egypt. It is the same bread in which the Hebrews shared with the angels, the ministering spirits of God.[61]

- ❖ Just as the hidden demons next to the altars of the nations

---

58 *Origen, Hom. in Luc.*, 23.
59 *Hom. in Num.*, 11,4).
60 *Comm. on Matt. 14:21 (ANF).*
61 *On Prayer 27:11 (ACW).*

used to feed on the smells of the sacrifices offered, so too the angels were drawn to the blood of the sacrifices presented by the children of Israel, as spiritual symbols and the smoke of incense, dwelling beside the altars and feeding on that kind of food.[62]

---

62   *De Principiis 1:8:1 (Cf. Butterworth).*

17

ORIGEN AND THE DEMONS

What is the goal of the demons?

Origen says that the Church affirms the existence of demons. They were rational beings who, due to their rejection of the Lord and disobedience to Him, became irrational, transforming from holy angels into fierce beasts. The devil and his angels represent forces of resistance to the holy life in the Lord. They fell and became opponents of divine truth.

Do demons have control over the righteous?

Origen wonders if the devil and his angels were destroyed by the work of Christ, why do we think that they still have the ability to control believers? In reality, their violent activity has an impact only on the wicked, and they do not have control over those who are in communion with the Lord Christ. We must realize that if a person becomes unworthy of a holy angel to accompany them, they surrender themselves to the devil because of their love for the sin they commit and their disobedience to the Lord. When the devil was light, before he went out of the Lord's obedience and fell into this state, turning his glory into dust, as the apostle says about him, he was called the "ruler of this world" (John 12:31), exercising his power over those who obey him and practice his evils. And since this world here does not mean the earthly place but rather the fall into the love of earthly things instead of heavenly things.

R. Cadiou says that the power of the devil appears in the weak soul lacking vigilance. The devil exploits its resistance due to a life of extravagance and laziness. He tries in every way to commit sins on a large scale. The devil knows how to benefit from sin, as he was the first sinner. He uses bodily temptations and evil thoughts, turning the fallen person into a murderer in anger, completely possessed by sin. Thus, the enemy of good incites sin, corrupting the purity of the soul. Sin finds its greatest opportunity in the body itself with its instincts that turn the soul away from the truth. There are evil germs inside the body that resist the good planted by the Lord in our minds. Therefore, the believer needs to seek divine grace for victory, as only the divine Savior can stand with the believer against the attacks of all the forces of hell.

Dominion and our control over demons

It is fitting for the believer before dominion to declare his rejection of the devil and all his thoughts.

The seeker of dominion heads west, towards the region of the devil to deny him, then heads east, to the land of salvation seeking God's grace and attaining dominion.

Origen warns of evil spirits lying in wait to lead humans away from God and towards the kingdom of darkness. Therefore, the believer must seek the help of God's grace to conquer the demons. Only our Christ is able to cleanse the wells of our souls filled with our sins, so that living waters can flow again. He affirms the permanence of God's grace in humans, despite the enemy's attempts to ensnare us.

Before we enjoyed faith, the kingdom of sin was within us. With the coming of our Savior Jesus, all evil spirits that invaded our hearts were destroyed, and He teaches us how to break them and not allow any of them to possess us, because if we leave any of them alive, we cannot resist evil, and the enemy of good remains dominant over us. This is what many of the fathers experienced, including the words of the apostolic Saint Athanasius: [Now, my beloved, the devil has been defeated, that tyrant who is against the whole world... he no longer has power over death, but life reigns instead of death, as the Lord says: "I am the life" (John 14:6), so that everything is filled with joy and happiness, as it is written: "The Lord has become king, let the earth rejoice"... Now that death has ceased, and the kingdom of the devil has crumbled, all are filled with joy and happiness!]

Saint Irenaeus says: [During the pains, the Lord ascended on high and led captivity captive, and gave gifts to men (Psalm 68:18; Ephesians 4:8), and granted those who believe in Him authority to tread on serpents and scorpions and all the power of the enemy, that is, authority over the leader of apostasy.] Saint John Chrysostom says: [What greater degradation than the devil who swelled up? And what height for man who desires to humble himself? The former crawls on the earth under our feet, while the latter ascends with the angels on high.] Origen says that whenever we read in the Gospels, we know perfectly well that we have the authority to tread (the devil) under our feet, this authority was not given to us in the old covenant, but in the new covenant. The Savior says: "Behold, I give you the authority to trample on serpents and scorpions, and over all the power of the enemy, and nothing shall by any means hurt you" (Luke 10:19). Our Lord Jesus came to crush all our enemies and deliver us from the snare of the devil.[63]

---

63 *In Matt. Hom. 56:6.*

What is the steadfast fatherhood, is it that of the devil or that of the Lord?

In the beginning, the devil was our father, this birth from the devil is severe misery. But the steadfast birth from the Lord is blessed. If you have the spirit of sonship and the Lord always saves you in every action and thought, and makes you steadfast in Jesus Christ. The Savior clearly demonstrates this in the Gospels when He says: "You are of your father the devil, and the desires of your father you want to do. He was a murderer from the beginning, and does not stand in the truth, because there is no truth in him. When he speaks a lie, he speaks from his own resources, for he is a liar and the father of it" (John 8:44). Therefore, if the seed of the Lord remains in us, when we keep the word of the Lord in us, we do not sin.

What is the danger of trusting in demons?

Origen sees in the Psalmist's saying: "A horse is a vain hope for safety; neither shall it deliver any by its great strength" (Psalm 33:17) a reference to those who trust in the devil and do not enjoy salvation. We pray to the true Lord and we are saved, while they pray to evil spirits that do not save them.

What are the currencies of the devil?

The currencies of the devil are murder, adultery, theft, false witness, greed, violence, and the like. All these are the riches of the devil, because such coins come from the circle of his money. With this kind of money, he buys his victims and makes slaves of all those who take money from his wealth.

What is the stance of demons towards the cross?

1. The demons, as princes of this world, thought that they had ensnared Jesus Christ and crucified Him, without knowing who was losing their power.

Through the cross, the dominion of demons was lost, and Satan was bound with a chain, and entered into his house, that is, hell. But if we follow Jesus, accept His words, and are filled with His faith, the demons become nothing in our sight.

What are the kingdoms of demons? What are their types?

Origen says: "Who is happier than man when he uproots the many kingdoms that Satan displays: the kingdoms of resisting forces, the kingdoms of sins, he uproots them through the words given to him by God, as it is written 'See, I have set my words in your mouth. See, I have appointed you this day over nations and over kingdoms to uproot.' And just as there are kingdoms, there are also peoples, for example, a kingdom of iniquity, and the peoples of iniquity represent the individual acts of iniquity. Greed and theft, which are sins of the same kind, represent only one kingdom, while there are several kingdoms, as there are various types of sins; look at sinners one by one until you realize what are the peoples subject to the kingdoms: we can say that this person, for example, has many peoples subject to the kingdom of iniquity, and another has many peoples subject to the kingdom of theft, or to the kingdom of condemnation or anger."

The word of God sent to these peoples and kingdoms works on uprooting and destruction. But what does it uproot? The Savior answered this question when He said, "Every plant that my heavenly Father has not planted will be pulled up" (Matthew 15:13). There are things inside souls that the heavenly Father has never planted: "evil thoughts, murder, adultery, sexual immorality, theft, false testimony, slander" (Matthew 15:19), all these plants that the heavenly Father has not planted. And if you want to know who planted these thoughts, listen: "An enemy did this" the one who "sowed weeds among the wheat." So God stands here then with His seed, and likewise the devil stands: if we leave "the house swept and put in order" for the devil, the enemy plants a plant that the heavenly Father has never planted, while if we leave the house swept and put in order for God instead of the devil, the Lord plants His seed with joy in our hearts. So do not think then that Jeremiah received a sad gift when he was appointed over nations and kingdoms to uproot. No, for God in His righteousness uproots evil with His word, uproots the enemy's kingdoms from the midst of the kingdom of heaven, uproots the peoples of the enemies from the midst of the people of God.[64]

---

64   Homilies on the Book of Jeremiah, Homily 2

18

ORIGEN AND THE TOLERANCE OF SINS

Jeremiah the prophet called us to learn from what my kingdoms of Israel and Judah did.

Origen in his fourth sermon on the book of Jeremiah explained the two verses: "The Lord said to me in the days of Josiah the king... The rebellious Israel has justified herself more than the treacherous Judah" (Jer 3:6, 11). [The prophet here wants us to know - as written in the book of Kings - that the people were divided in the days of Rehoboam into a kingdom consisting of ten tribes under the rule of Jeroboam (the kingdom of Israel), and into another kingdom consisting of two tribes under the rule of Rehoboam (the kingdom of Judah)... Israel, under Jeroboam and his successors, sinned first, and its sins compared to Judah reached a point where God made them be taken into captivity by the Assyrians.

God says: "I divorced Israel first because of her sins and sent her away from me, and Judah did not return to me despite knowing what happened to Israel", he also speaks of our sins. When we read about the calamities and horrors that befell the people of Israel, we should be filled with awe and say: "If God did not spare the natural branches, perhaps he will not spare you either" (Rom 11:21). If those who boast of being true olive branches, rooted in the lineage of Abraham, Isaac, and Jacob, were cut off by God without mercy, despite his righteousness and love for humanity, then how much more us? "Behold the kindness and severity of God" (Rom 11:22), for he is not kind without severity, nor severe without kindness. If God were only kind without severity, we would increase in contempt and indifference towards his kindness. And if he were severe without kindness, we would fall into despair because of our sins. But in reality, since he is God, he is kind and severe at the same time, and as humans, we choose his kindness if we return to him, and we choose his severity if we remain in our sins. God speaks to us through the prophets to say: "Have you seen what the rebellious Israel did" (Jer 3:6), Israel here understood as the Jewish people, "they went to every high mountain and every green tree" (worshipping idols and committing adultery).

If you look at the Pharisee who arrogantly went up to the temple without beating his chest or realizing his sins, but rather said: "God, I thank you that I am not like the rest of the people, extortioners, unjust, adulterers, or like this tax collector. I fast twice a week and pay tithes of everything I get" (If 18: 11-12), you will understand that he ascended to every high mountain, with his blameworthy feelings and his love of boasting and boasting, and likewise with vanity and pride he also ascended to every high hill. He came under every tree, not a fruitful tree, but only a tree of wood. There is a difference between wood trees and fruit trees: when we plant wood trees only, we are planting non-fruiting seeds, just deep seeds. It symbolizes the dialogues of heretics and their veils, which have a deceitful, deceptive luster that is not suitable for convincing the listeners. If we leave ourselves behind these arguments, we go under every tree for wood. "There she committed adultery. After she had done all this, I said to her, 'Return to me.' But she did not return. She saw her traitorous sister Judah (betrayal of Israel)." This reproach is also directed at us, we who sin and do not fulfill our covenants with God, we who do not see what happened to those who lost their covenants with God despite being descendants of Abraham and despite having received the promise.

We must then hold on to this thought: Since these were cut off from divine blessings and promises, and being descendants of Abraham did nothing to benefit them, how much more, if we have sinned, will we be neglected by God. The Savior tells us: "If you were Abraham's children, you would do the works of Abraham." Saint John also says to them: "Do not begin to say within yourselves, 'We have Abraham as our father,' for I tell you that God is able from these stones to raise up children for Abraham." By these stones, he means us, with our stony hearts and our hardness toward the truth, and it is indeed a fact that God, in His power, raised children to Abraham through the stones.

"Then I saw that for all reasons, since the transgressor Israel had committed adultery, I divorced her, and I gave her a certificate of divorce. The traitorous sister, Judah, did not fear." After all that she had done to Israel, Judah was not afraid of what happened to the others.][1]

---

1 See Homily 4, translated by Jacqueline Samir Kosti.

19

ORIGEN AND THE ECCLESIASTICAL MAN

The priest and the philosopher

Origen is considered a "church man," in all that this expression carries in meaning. He was proud to be churchly. It can be said that the Bible and the Church were the foundation of all his writings and sermons, and he was the first to address the criticism of the texts of the Old Testament, as well as dealt with the theological issues related to the relationship between the old and new covenants, thus presenting the ecclesiastical tradition.[2]

John Daniel calls Origen "the church man," saying: "We have seen in the story of his life how he was a teacher of the educated, a lecturer, a priest, a theologian, and a martyr successively; that is, he spent his entire life in accomplishing churchly works." Jaroslav Pelikan says: One of the most important differences between the theologian and the philosopher, which is settled between them, is that the former

---

2 *Thomas Halton: The Church (Message of the Fathers of the Church, vol. 4, p. 21.)*

considers himself, in a traditional expression of Origen, as a "church man," speaking on behalf of the Christian community. Even in his theological ideas and in his arguments regarding what was called public teaching in the church at that time, Origen realized as a theologian that he was responsible for preserving the Christian proclamation and the continuous authority of the church. His personal opinions were respected, as they were considered a development of what the church believes in, teaches, and confesses, based on the word of God.[3] As for philosophers like Justinus, Tatian, Clemens, and others similar to them, they converted to Christianity and remained philosophers. Origen, when he declared himself in love as a "church man," affirmed what was born in him, and that this is the fundamental characteristic of all his genius. When he spoke about the world, he used this word in its Gospel meaning, the perishable world, especially the evil world from which our Lord Jesus came to liberate us. Origen always resorts to the judgment of the church and its faith, preaching, and tradition of its creed. He sees in the bones of the Passover lamb, which cannot be broken, a symbol of the church's beliefs that nothing will be broken from them, and he wishes that there be no difference in doctrine[4] among the churches. He is a resolute man of iron in faith. He is not concerned with his insignificance, for his angel sees the face of the Father.[5]

Concepts of the Church in Origen

The Church is the house of God: It was the first to declare that the Church is the city of God on earth,[6] living forever, alongside the civil state.[7] It says: "Christ describes the Church as the house of God. And the Apostle Paul teaches, saying: If I stay in it for a long time,

---

3   Jean Daniélou: Origen, NY, 1955, p. 27.
4   Jaroslav Pelikan: The Christian Tradition, 1. The Emergence of the Catholic Tradition.
5   Henri De Lubac: Origen, On First Principles, NY., 1966 (Koetschau text together with an introduction and notes by G.W. Butterworth, p. X, XIII.
6   In Jer. hom. 9.2; In Jos. hom. 8.7.
7   Quasten, p. 82.

this is so that you may know how to behave in the house of the Lord, which is his Church, the pillar of truth and its foundation. So if the Church is the house of God, and because everything that belongs to the Father belongs to the Son, then the Church is therefore the house of the Son of God.[8] *And he speaks of the Church as the spiritual temple of God, saying: [The Spirit of Christ dwells in those who are like him, I say in terms of appearance and characteristics, so much so that the word of God (the Lord Christ) wants to clarify this matter for us clearly, as God presents in his promises to the righteous "I will dwell in them and walk among them, and I will be their God, and they will be my people" (2 Cor 6:16, Lev 26:12, Zech 8:8). And the Savior says: "If anyone loves me, he will keep my word, and my Father will love him, and we will come to him and make our home with him" (John 14:23). In other parts of the Bible, he speaks of the mystery of resurrection for those whose ears have been opened by God, saying that the temple that was destroyed will be rebuilt anew from living and precious stones. This makes us understand that all those led by the word of God to strive together on the path of piety are precious stones in the great one temple of God.*[9] *Origen was impressed by the position of the people of God towards the building of the temple, as each person was enthusiastic to generously offer all that was within their capabilities according to their abilities and resources. He experienced his role in urging himself to contribute to the establishment of the spiritual temple of God within him, saying: [O Lord Jesus Christ, make me worthy to participate in the building of your house. Let us build the temple of the God of Jacob, Jesus our Lord, and adorn it. The dwelling place of God is holiness... And thus each of us can prepare a tent for God in our hearts. Its ten compartments (Exodus 26:1) refer to the implementation of the Ten Commandments.]*[10]

Origen calls the Church the "city of God," as it is "the dwelling of

---

8   Comm. on the Songs of Songs, book 3:3 (ACW).
9   Contra Celsus 8:28,29.
10 In Exod. hom. 13:9.

God with the people" (Rev 3:21). God builds his Church as his own city, not with stones, but with his chosen believers.

The Church is the assembly of believers: Origen describes the Church as the assembly of believers served by the priests.[11]

1. **The Church is the house of faith: The only Son himself expressed his admiration for the faith of the people (Matt 10:8); while he did not admire gold or wealth or earthly kingdoms, for nothing equals the value of faith.**[12]

2. **The Church, the Bride of Christ: The school of Alexandria, especially Origen in his interpretation of the Song of Songs, adopted this Gospel concept of the Church as a heavenly bride of Christ. [Do not think that the bride, that is, the Church, did not exist until after the resurrection of the Savior; she existed before the foundation of the world (Ephesians 4:1).**[13]

3. **The Church, the Body of Christ: The believer who belongs to it is like a member of this body.**[14] **[The Bible declares to us that the Church of God as a whole is the body of Christ, living by the Son of God. And the members of this body are the believers. Just as the soul gives life to the body, which in itself has no natural power to move, so it is with regard to the Word that activates each member belonging to it, so that they do not do anything outside the Word.]**[15]

4. *The Church, the House of Salvation: The Church is the ark of salvation, receiving light from Jesus Christ, and has the ability to interpret the Bible. [The sign of salvation (the scarlet cord) was given through a window, because Christ in His incarnation gave*

---

11 *Against Celsus 8:75; in Jer. hom. 11:3.*
12 *In Matt 10:19.*
13 *Comm. on Cant. 11:8 (ACW 26:149; tr. R.P. Lawson).*
14 *Against Celsus 6:48; in Matt. 14:17.*
15 *Contra Cels. 6,48 ANF.*

us a vision of the light of divinity as through a window, so that everyone may obtain salvation through that sign, which will be found in a house that was once a harlot, then purified by water and the Spirit, and by the blood of our Lord and Savior Jesus Christ, to whom be glory and power forever. Amen.][16] *[Jesus came "for the falling and rising of many" (Luke 2:34). For those who deny His sign, His blood is directed towards punishment, but for those who believe, it is for salvation. Therefore, outside this house, that is, outside the Church, no one will be saved. If a person forsakes it, he bears the responsibility for his death.]*[17]

5. **The Church has the authority of forgiveness of sins, says Origen: [Just as the sun and the moon illuminate our bodies, so do our minds illuminate with Christ and the Church.]**[18]

6. **The Church, a community of love: Origen speaks of the love that unites the earth with heaven. [One of the great virtues is that we love one another. And we must believe that the saints who have departed have that love towards those who are struggling in the battle of life, to a degree far exceeding those who are still subject to human weakness, and busy with the struggle of their weaker brothers. For the words, "If one member suffers, all the members suffer with it. If one member is honored, all the members rejoice with it" (1 Corinthians 12:26) are not limited to those who love their brothers on earth. If the angels of God came to Jesus and served Him (Matthew 4:11), and if we believe that this angelic service was not limited to the short period of His earthly journey, how many angels, in your opinion, serve Jesus.]**[19]

---

16   *In Lib. Issu Nave 3:5(Battenson, p. 3360-7).*
17   *In Josh. hom 3:5.*
18   *In Gen. hom. 1:7.*
19   *On Prayer 11:2.*

7. **The Church Zion Gates:** The church is the gate of righteousness, through which Jesus Christ enters the gate. The gates of the church are located in the opposite direction of the gates of death. [The gates of Zion can be understood as opposed to the gates of death. There is therefore one gate for death and sin, while the gate of Zion is self-control. This is what the prophet means when he says: "This is the gate of the Lord, through which the righteous enter" (Psalm 21:118). There is also cowardice, which is a gate to death, and courage is the gate of Zion... In contrast to all the gates of false knowledge, there is one gate in front of it, the gate of knowledge free from lies. But if we consider that "our struggle is not against flesh and blood" (Ephesians 12:6), we say that all the power of the ruler of the world is darkness, and the "spiritual forces of evil in the heavenly realms" (Ephesians 12:6) is the gate of hell.[20]

8. *The New Israel: Origen sees that the Israelites are no longer Israel according to history, while the believers of the nations have become the New Israel, which requires a redefinition of Israel.*[21]

9. **The Church as Noah's Ark**[22] **and the Mystery of Forgiveness:** Origen interprets Noah's ark and its dimensions symbolically, as the Church of Christ. [Regarding the width of the ark, the number 50 is mentioned, which is a sacred number symbolizing forgiveness and reconciliation. According to the law, there was a specific time for debt forgiveness, which was once every fifty years. And now Christ, the spiritual Noah in his ark, is the Church in which the human race is saved from destruction.][23] Origen says: [The number 50 includes the mystery of

---

20   *Commentary on Matthew, Book 12:13 (Cf. ANF).*
21   N.R.M. De Lange: *Origen and the Jews: Studies in Jewish-Christian Relations in Third-Century Palestine*, 1976, Cambridge, p. 80.
22   Jean Daniélou: *The Bible and the Liturgy*, p.325-7.
23   *In Gen. hom. 2:5.*

forgiveness... The fiftieth day after Easter is a feast according to the law, and the same in the Gospel. In the parable of forgiveness and pardon, the Lord speaks of the debtor of fifty denarii.][24]

10. **The Church as Our Mother:** [According to the spirit, your Father is God, and your Mother is the heavenly Jerusalem (Galatians 26:4; Hebrews 22:12). Learn this from the testimonies of the prophets and apostles. Moses included this meaning in his song: "Is He not your Father who bought you?!" (Deuteronomy 6:32).][25] [The apostle says about the heavenly Jerusalem that she is our mother, she is free (Galatians 26:4). Your Father is the God who begot your spirit, saying "I have raised sons and brought them up" (Isaiah 2:1). And Paul says: "Should we not submit very much to the Father of spirits so that we may live?!" (Hebrews 9:12).][26]

11. **The Church as an interpreter of the Holy Scriptures:** [We must explain to the believers how the sacred scriptures are not the works of the law, but were placed and revealed to us by the inspiration of the Holy Spirit, by the will of the Father of the universe, through Jesus Christ. This is in addition to the various methods of interpretation that appear and are carried out in accordance with the divine law of Jesus Christ, through the succession of the apostles.][27] Origen believes that the presence of the Lord Jesus Christ in the midst of His people in the Church enlightens their inner eyes. [If you desire it, in this church, and in this congregation, your eyes will see the Lord. For when you raise your noblest thoughts to contemplate the wisdom and truth, which is the only begotten Son of the Father, you will see Jesus with your eyes. Blessed is the congregation about which

---

24 *In Num. hom.* 5:2; see also 25:2.
25 *Homilies on Leviticus* 9:9 (Cf. Frs. of the Church)
26 *Homilies on Leviticus* 11:3 (Cf. Frs. of the Church)
27 *De Principiis* 4:2 (Henri De Lubac).

it is written that the eyes of all believers and catechumens, men and women, and children, have seen Jesus, not with physical eyes, but with those of the spirit.][28]

12. **The Church, the adornment and light of the world:** [The adornment of the world is the Church adorned with Jesus, the light of the world.][29] The Church, in imitating her bridegroom, is the light of the world. Origen calls on his opponents to compare between the pagan lands and the Christian churches that emerged in them. If the churches formed by Christ are compared to the city assemblies, they will appear as shining beacons in the world. [The Church of God in Athens is precious and steadfast, exerting all efforts to please the Most High God, while the Athenian assemblies are noisy and turbulent, and cannot be compared to the Church in any way.][30]

Features of the Church

1. **One Church:** Origen sees the unity of the Church built on the foundation of its one faith and its one system and administration. "I carry the title of priest as you see, so I preach the word of God. But if I act contrary to the system of the Church or the rules established by the Gospel, or if I wrong you or the Church, I hope that the Church will unite in one opinion and expel me. In the ninth sermon on the book of Joshua,[31] Origen speaks of the temple of God, in which Jesus Christ can offer his sacrifice to the Father. It is built of pure, unbroken stones. "No iron tool has been used" (see Deut 5:27). These are the living, pure stones, the holy apostles who compose one temple through the unity of their hearts (Acts 24:1) and souls. They

---

28   *In Luc. hom.* 32:6 *(Thomas K. Carroll; Messages of the Fathers of the Church).*
29   *Comm. on John, book 6:38.*
30   *Contra Celsum 3:27.*
31   *In Jos. hom.* 7:6; *Jean Daniélou: Origen, NY, 1955, p. 8.*

were devoted to prayer with one mind (Acts 14:1), as they had one mind. True unity, founded on holy life, love, common worship, and one faith. Origen considers the sanctification of each member as the foundation of the Church's unity, as what one member does affects others. He says, "One wrongdoer defiles the people."[32]

2. **The Church includes believers of different degrees:** "There are among Christians in the Church those who are true believers, who believe in God and do not question His commandments. They perform their religious duties and desire to serve, but they are not pure in their behavior and private lives. They do not put off the old self with its practices (Col 3:9). They are like the Gibeonites, wearing their worn-out clothes and sandals (Josh 9:5)." The same applies to our church rituals, some things that everyone must practice, even though some do not understand them. For example, why do we kneel during prayer? Or why do we face east? And who can easily explain the sanctity of the Eucharist sacrament, or partake in it; or reveal the mysteries behind the texts of the baptism sacrament and its rituals, questions, and answers? Nevertheless, we carry all these things, they are veiled and covered over our shoulders, and we do them as handed down to us by our high priest (the Lord Christ) and his children.

Origen also explains the presence of wicked people in the Church. "We see our assemblies also filled with the wicked. Our hope is that those who are cast into the fire will outnumber the righteous."

3. **The Church loves all of humanity:** Facing accusations that Christians believe that God abandoned all humans and became

---

32 *In Jos. hom. 7. PG 12:861, 244.*

interested only in the Church, Origen responded that this is not a Christian doctrine.[33]

4. **The Church enjoys life after the resurrection of Jesus:** United with the risen Christ, the Church is called to shine in greater splendor and glory, as if perfection has been achieved. [Arise, my love, my beautiful one, and come away. For behold, the winter is past; the rain is over and gone. The flowers appear on the earth (Song of Solomon 2:10-12). We can say that this was like a prophecy directed towards the Church, inviting it to the blessings promised by the Lord in the future. You have been called to "arise," as if the time of perfection has come, and the resurrection has arrived. Issuing this command was like a seal on the work of the resurrection, more glorious and radiant.][34]

5. **The Church mourns for sinners:** The Church will remain with its head, our Lord Jesus, in sorrow until sinners return to their God and submit to the Father. Origen comments on the words, "I tell you I will not drink again of this fruit of the vine until that day when I drink it new with you in my Father's kingdom" (Matthew 26:29), saying that wine in the Bible symbolizes spiritual joy. God has promised His people that He will bless them with wine, meaning He will give them abundance of spiritual joy. The saints do not receive their full rewards for their merits immediately upon leaving this world, they await us even though we may be delayed. They do not have complete joy while mourning for our sins and transgressions.

6. **The Church lives in unceasing victory:** The members of the Church crush all evil forces with divine grace, and even the gates of hell will not prevail against them. [He encourages his

---

33 *Contra Celsus 4:28; N.R.M. De Lange: Origen and the Jews: Studies in Jewish-Christian Relations in Third-Century Palestine, 1976, Cambridge, p. 76.*
34 *Commentary on the Song of Songs 3.14; ACW 26.239, 245.*

Church to tread on traps and trample snares, then joyfully say: "Our soul has escaped as a bird from the snare of the fowlers; the snare is broken, and we have escaped" (Psalm 124:7). Who tore apart the traps if not the One who cannot be caught? Although he suffered death, it was by his will, not as it happens to us because of our sins. He alone has become free among the dead. And since he is alive among the dead, when he destroyed death, the one who had the power of death, and brought those who tasted death.]

7. **The Church never ceases to preach throughout the world:** The Church, as seen and loved by Origen, remains always a community of Christ's disciples spread throughout the earth.[35]

8. **The Church is old and new:** The Church is new in her life in Christ, as she accepts the work of the Holy Spirit who renews our thoughts and our lives without ceasing. It is also very ancient, as it exists in the mind of God who planned our salvation, before the foundation of the world. [The Apostle says that the Church was built on a foundation not only of the Apostles but also of the Prophets (Ephesians 2:20). Adam is considered among the prophets, as he prophesied about that great mystery, with regard to Christ and the Church, when he said, "Therefore a man will leave his father and his mother and cling to his wife, and they will become one flesh" (Genesis 2:24). As for the Apostle, it is clear that he is speaking with regard to Christ and the Church when he says "This mystery is great, but I speak with regard to Christ and the church" (Ephesians 5:32). He also says: "Just as Christ also loved the church, and gave himself up for her, that he might sanctify her, cleansing her with the washing of water" (Ephesians 5:25). -26).][36]

---

35 R. Cadiou: *Origen, Herder Book Co., 1944, p. 313.*
36 *Comm. on Cant. Cant. 2[Bettenson: Early Christian Fathers, 1956, p. 338-9].*

[Tell me, you who only come to church on a holiday, are the rest of the days not holidays? True Christians partake daily of the body of the Lamb, that is, they eat daily the body of the Word.][37]

Will all the rest of Israel believe after all nations accept faith in Jesus Christ?

Origen says: [Perhaps we, who come from the nations, know that with the fall of Israel, the way to salvation has opened for us, and the Jews have been expelled so that we may enter in their place. On the other hand, since we know that hardness has come upon Israel partially until the fullness of the nations enters. And so all Israel will be saved (Romans 11:25), let us explain the meaning of the statement made by Saint Paul the Apostle, what is meant by all Israel will be saved when the fullness of the nations enters? There was a remnant in Israel for salvation: if the majority of Israel has fallen, but a remnant has obtained it by grace (Romans 11:5), the remnant spoken of in Elijah: "I have reserved for Myself seven thousand men who have not bowed the knee to Baal." And in explaining the meaning of this remnant, Paul the Apostle says: "Even so then, at this present time there is a remnant according to the election of grace" (Romans 11:5). Therefore, there was a remnant in Israel for salvation when Israel was rejected. The Apostle did not say, "When all the nations are saved, then all Israel will be saved," but rather, "Until the fullness of the nations enters. And so all Israel will be saved."][38]

Church tradition

Origen was strongly committed to ecclesiastical tradition, and he tried to use philosophy in his interpretation. He says: "We affirm that what

---

37 Ibid. 10.3 (Heine, 162-63)
38 Origen, Homilies on the Book of Jeremiah, Homily 5:4, translated by Jacqueline Samir Kosti.

we believe as truth does not contradict in any way with the tradition of the Church."[39] It is the decisive standard for the apostolic continuity to define doctrine in the universal Church. Saint Paul says: "O Timothy, guard the deposit" (1 Tim 6:20), as it is an acceptance of Christ himself, and the Holy Spirit in him. [It is our duty to be cautious not to use this sacred deposit in a defiled manner when sin leads us to accept it, thus confirming that we have not received this deposit. Surely, if it were within us, we would not have accepted sin. It is necessary to connect the vision of the word of God with action, as it says: "as servants of the word."[40] Knowledge and practical life go hand in hand. Origen also says that actions are the crown of knowledge.[41]

Ecclesiastical Discipline

"It has become customary in the Church of Christ to exclude those who openly practice sins from common prayer,"[42] fearing that the little leaven may spoil those who are unable to pray with pure hearts. Church leaders must exclude sinners of bad reputation from participating in the Eucharist. It is the duty of the good shepherd to exclude the black sheep from his flock, otherwise its infection will spread to the other sheep. However, leaders must exercise this authority with moderation. [43]It is advisable for them to see if they can absolve them through advice or reprimand before deciding to exclude them from participating in the Church. The Church can accept back into its membership a Christian who was previously deprived, if they show true repentance and a firm resolve not to return to sin.[44]

---

39 *De Principiis, I. praef. 2.*
40 *Jaroslav Pelikan : The Christian Tradition, Chicago, 1971, p. 115.*
41 *Homilies on Leviticus 4:3. (See Frs. of the Church)*
42 *In Mattthaem Commentariorum Series, 89 PG 13:1740; Ernest Latko: Origen's Concept of penance, Laval 1949, p. 89.*
43 *Fragm. on 1 Corinthians, ed. by C. Jenkins, Journal of Theological Studies (1908): 364.*
44 *Comm. on Matt. 16:8.*

Discipline and the Degrees of Believers

Discipline should be stricter and firmer according to the responsibility of the believer in the Church and their role in it. [The admonished deserves more mercy than the believer. And the deacon has more right to forgiveness than the priest.][45] Origen emphasizes not to start with public discipline, but to communicate with the wrongdoer in a way that does not hurt their feelings so that they can correct their situation and not be pushed to justify their mistake. Origen warns against using the power of deprivation against the sinner, saying: "But it must be used rarely."[46]

Origen explains that it is fitting for bishops to expect insults from those who impose deprivation on them. And it is our duty not to listen to rumors filled with malicious exaggerations, spread by those who have been cut off, with the aim of hurting the bishop with their sharp tongues.[47] [Prophets and teachers endure what doctors endure from unwilling patients who refuse harsh medical treatment. Like these undisciplined patients, they either try to escape from their doctors, or direct harm and insults towards them, treating them as if they were enemies.][48]

[Purification from sin is not achieved through physical punishment, but through repentance.][49]

---

45   *In Ezech. hom. 5:4*; Jean Daniélou: *Origen*, NY, 1955, p. 25.
46   *In Mattaeum Commentarii Liber 25, Liber 16:8 PG 13:1396*; Ernest Latko: *Origen's Concept of penance*, Laval 1949, p. 98.
47   *In Jer. hom. 14:14*; Ernest Latko: *Origen's Concept of penance*, Laval 1949, p. 94.
48   *In Jer. hom. 14:1*.
49   *Homilies on Leviticus 11:1 (Cf. Frs. of the Church)*

The Priesthood and the People

The priests are successors to the apostles: Origen combined the apostolic and priestly definitions in Christian ministry by saying: [The apostles and their successors, the priests, following the pattern of the high priest, guided by the Holy Spirit, discern which sins they offer their sacrifices for, when they offer them, and how.][50]

The priests as interpreters of the holy books: Origen believed that the main tasks of the priests of the Old Covenant were to perform ritual services, while teaching was the fundamental message of the priests of the New Covenant. Origen found joy in the priesthood of the Old Covenant, as the priests were primarily dedicated to serving God. After his return to Alexandria from his first trip to Caesarea, Origen wrote about this in the introduction to "Commentary on the Gospel of John." He explained that the priests were dedicated to studying the word of God, and the high priests were those who excelled in this field. There is no doubt that these ranks correspond to the ecclesiastical ranks, as the priests, especially the high priest, also have the privilege of standing before God. In this, Origen follows the footsteps of Clement of Alexandria in considering the priest as a spiritual person. However, the priest's privilege of approaching the divine mysteries is only for the purpose of fulfilling his mission as a teacher, mediating the delivery of the word of God to others. Origen transforms the Jewish ritual law into an explanation of the priest's calling as a teacher. For example, he sees the removal of the skin from the sacrifice as a symbol of excluding the literal meaning from the word of God, and taking pure incense in hand as a symbol of precise distinction in the field of explanation and interpretation of difficult paragraphs. He also interprets the sacrifice itself as a continuous liberation of the soul from the body, making it possible to perceive higher truths.

---

50 *On Prayer, 28:9; Jaroslav Pelikan : The Christian Tradition, Chicago, 1971, p. 59.*

Accordingly, the Levitical priesthood came to symbolize an ethical and cultural elite of inspired teachers in the field of studying the Holy Scriptures. This transformation reaches its peak in Origen's interpretation of the garments of the high priest, where each piece symbolizes one of the spiritual qualifications.[51] If the apostle is an inspired interpreter, he is also, like the priest, responsible for delivering the word of God to people at different levels of spiritual progress. Jesus Christ made this clear in his command to his disciples to allow children to come to him, expressing the advanced Christian commitment to descend to the simple.[52] "The Acts of the Apostles" are actually "Acts of Teaching," for when Jesus entrusted his disciples, giving them the authority to heal the blind and raise the dead, he had in mind a reconsideration of those "blinded" by corrupt teachings and the resurrection of those who "died" in their sins.[53] Apostleship is a mission that is accomplished through action. Bishops occupy a place in divine administration, sharing the responsibility of caring for their dioceses with the angelic bishops who assist them.[54] As a result of these unique responsibilities, bishops have been given greater authority than ordinary Christians, so what is expected of them - in terms of obligations - is greater in return.[55] [Moses knew from personal experience that Joshua was skilled in the law and knowledge, which made the children of Israel obedient to him. And since these matters are full of secrets, we cannot ignore what is most precious, even if their literalness may seem necessary and useful.][56] [Christ teaches and seeks his tools that he uses to spread his teaching. I pray that I may be

---

51 *Church History 50 (1981) : The Charismatic Intellectual: Origen's Understanding of Religious Leadership*, p. 111-112.
52 *Comm. on Matt.* 15:7.
53 *In Isaiah hom.* 6:4.
54 *De Principiis* 1:8:1; *In Luke hom.* 12:3.
55 *In Jerm. hom* 11:3; *Fragm.* 50.
56 *In Num. hom.* 22:4; *Church History 50 (1981): The Charismatic Intellectual: Origen's Understanding of Religious Leadership*, p. 116.

ready for that, proclaiming my submission to him.]⁵⁷ The primary characteristic of the apostle's mission as a teacher and interpreter of the Holy Scriptures is his duty to exercise discernment. Here, Paul, the greatest of the apostles, provided Origen with a similar example regarding apostolic discernment when he boldly extracted from the storehouses "the hidden wisdom of God in a mystery" (1 Cor 2:7), distinguishing between spiritual Christians. As for the simple among them, he ruled that it was appropriate for them to know nothing except Jesus Christ, and him crucified (1 Cor 2:2).⁵⁸

Origen was keen on the apostles, as with the priests. For the apostles are the ones who carry out the work of the apostle, such as revisiting those who have been blinded by corrupt teachings, and raising those who have died in their sins to life.⁵⁹ Apostleship is realized through its fruits, or as Paul said: "If I am not an apostle to others, yet doubtless I am to you. For you are the seal of my apostleship" (1 Cor 9:2).⁶⁰

What are the characteristics of the priest and his family?

It was said of Zechariah the priest and his wife Elizabeth, who were both descendants of Aaron, "They were both righteous before God, walking in all the commandments and ordinances of the Lord blameless" (Luke 1:6). Origen explained this by saying: [A person may not find anything to accuse me of after examining me, for I am blameless before people... But the judgment of people is not correct, for they do not know if I have ever sinned in secret within my heart, and they do not know if I have looked at a woman and desired her and lived in the adultery of the heart. People may see me giving to the best of my ability, but they do not know if I do it for the sake of God's command or to seek the

---

57 *In Luc. hom. 32:2.*
58 *See Comm. on John 13:18; Hom. on Lev. 4:6.*
59 *Hom. on Isa. 6:4.*
60 *Comm. on John 32:17; Joseph Wilson Trigg: Origen, SCM Press, 1985, p. 142.*

praise of people... Blessed is the person who is righteous before God, and who is praised by God, for man is incapable of judging with justice and clarity. People may praise those who do not deserve praise, and condemn those who do not deserve condemnation. Only God is just in praise and condemnation.][61]

Origen also comments on the expression "blameless," saying: [It was said of the church that it is "glorious, not having spot or wrinkle" (Eph 5:27). This does not mean that the children of the church have never sinned, but rather they live a life of repentance. The expression "without wrinkle" means his disdain for the old man and his abstaining from sin, hence the phrase "to be holy and without blemish," for the soul has inherited sin, but it becomes pure without blame if the filth of sin is removed from it.][62]

The priesthood and the ability to teach.

It is not enough for the priest to be characterized by wisdom and understanding, but also to have the ability to convey what he knows to others.[63] The priest wears the "garment of teaching" when instructing the advanced in faith, and the "garment of the word" for teaching beginners.[64] In commenting on the priest's attire inside and outside the Holy of Holies, it is said: "You see this great priest in his knowledge, when he is inside among the perfect as in the 'Holy of Holies,' how he wears the 'garment of teaching.' But when he goes out to those who do not have this ability, he exchanges it for the garment of the word, and teaches simpler matters, giving some 'milk' 'like children' (1 Cor 3: 1-2), and to the weak a word, and to others different ones he gives strong food (Rom 14: 2). "But solid food is for the mature, who because of practice have their senses trained to discern good and evil" (Heb 5:

---

61   *In Luc. hom 2: 3.*
62   *In Luc. hom 2: 12.*
63   *In Lev. hom. 6:4.*
64   *In Lev. hom. 4:6.*

14). The Apostle Paul knows how to change clothes, using one garment with the people and another in the service of the sacred.[65]

Priests and teachers as pillars of the church

Just as the tent of meeting in the Old Covenant was connected by intertwined pillars, so do teachers in the church assist members as partners in the community, being their right hand... Let the pillars be overlaid with silver, for those who proclaim the word of God receive through the Holy Spirit "the word of the Lord" which is "pure like silver refined in a furnace" (Psalm 12: 6). But they have prophets as a basis for their proclamation, while the crossbars between the pillars are the right hands of the mutual apostolic membership. Let the curtains be sewn with loops, hung in circles, and tied with threads, to be spread out in a way that the house is twenty-eight cubits long and four cubits wide. This is how the remaining remnant of the congregation, who cling and hold onto the ropes of faith, is gathered, as "the threefold cord is not quickly broken" (Ecclesiastes 4: 12). This is faith in the Holy Trinity, by which the church is connected and strengthened... The ten hallways have been built to accommodate the total number of perfection, and refer to the Ten Commandments in the Law. As for the purple, blue, scarlet, and fine linen, they indicate various achievements. They reveal outer and inner curtains, and all the priestly garments overlaid with gold and adorned with jewels.[66]

The progression of strength[67]

Origen says, "He is an example of the image (of Christ) who bestowed priesthood upon the church, taking on the sins of the people as priests

---

65 *Homilies on Leviticus 4:6. (See Frs. of the Church)*
66 *In Exodus hom. 9:3 (Cf. Ronad E Heine- Frs. of the Church, vol. 71.)*
67 *Ernest Latko: Origen's Concept of penance, Laval 1949, p. 72 f.*

and servants of the church, they grant forgiveness in imitation of their Lord."[68]

In a sermon on one of the Psalms, Origen pointed to the great authority of the bishops by saying, "Christ was the great physician who could heal every disease and weakness. And now His apostles Peter and Paul, like the prophets, are also physicians. Following their example, those who are established after them in the affairs of the church are also given the gifts of healing from wounds. These are the servants whom God has established as doctors for souls in the church.[69]

The Inner Priesthood

The hierarchical order in the church is not understood as a visible priesthood, but according to the degree of inner perfection. What benefit is it if I occupy the first place in the congregation and hold the honor of presidency, if I do not have deeds that make me deserving of this dignity?![70]

The Authority and Purity

Origen affirms that the legitimacy of the ecclesiastical authority depends on the state of the priest's soul. [If his personal sins bind him tightly, there is no room for him to exercise the authority of absolution and binding."] Origen also emphasizes the importance of spiritual qualities in bishops, believing that a wrong bishop loses his authority over the forgiveness of sins. He says, "Let us contemplate the meaning of what was said to Peter, and to any Peter among the believers: 'I will give you the keys of the kingdom of heaven' (Matt 16:19). For whoever judges unjustly, and does not bind on earth according to the will of Christ,

---

68   *In Lev. hom 5:3.*
69   *In Psalm. 37 hom 1:1 PG 12:1369;* Ernest Latko: *Origen's Concept of penance,* Laval 1949, p. 74.
70   *In Ezek. Hom. 5:4. PG 13:707.*

the gates of hell prevail against him. But they will not prevail against those who judge justly, and possess the keys of the kingdom of heaven, opening its doors to those who are 'loosed' on earth, so that they also become loosed and free in heaven. And closed to those who judge against him justly, binding on earth, so that they also become 'bound' in heaven. If those who receive the rank of bishopric use this text as Peter did, affirming that they receive the keys of the kingdom of heaven from Christ, and that what they loose on earth is loosed in heaven, and what they bind on earth is bound in heaven, their claim is true if they live their lives in accordance with that, and in line with what was said that Christ built the church on them, the gates of hell will not prevail against them in exercising the authority of absolution and binding. But if they are bound by the ropes of their sins, there is no place for them to exercise this authority."[71]

Bishops and False Glory

In Origen's commentary on Joshua and his behavior in obtaining his inheritance, after all the tribes, and even after Caleb, he says: [Why did he make himself the last of all? So that he may become the first of them (Matt 19:30). His inheritance was not obtained by his own decision, but by the people, as the Holy Scripture states, "The children of Israel gave Joshua the son of Nun a portion among them" (Josh 19:49). But now "these things happened to them as examples" (1 Cor 10:11). For as it is said, if you walk in humility, your worth increases, and you gain favor from the Lord (Sirach 3:17). Also: "If they choose you as a leader over them, do not be arrogant but be one among them as one of them" (Sirach 32:10).][72]

Origen presented a picture of himself as an example of the clergy and teachers not losing their way:

---

[71] *Ernest Latko: Origen's Concept of penance, Laval 1949, p. 70.*
[72] *In Jos. hom. 24:2.*

A. He attributed the credit for his understanding and familiarity with the Holy Scriptures to the grace of God, not to himself.

B. On many occasions, he would urge those attending his meetings to also listen to those who were wiser than him, and to those whom God had blessed with greater understanding. [Perhaps there is another person wiser than me, and considered by God worthy to enjoy the revelation and wisdom in interpreting with the Spirit of God, and to receive the gift of knowing the Word with the Spirit (1 Cor 8:12). He may present a better interpretation than me, even though I have exerted all my efforts.][73] Origen humbly concludes his interpretations, saying: [This is the most I can accomplish, may someone capable of receiving greater grace to understand this passage speak with more and better words.] Origen demands humility from the clergy, following the example of the great Moses among the prophets, who did not dare to choose a successor for himself, but asked God to choose someone suitable for this position.[74]

The priesthood and commerce in the house of the Lord: Let every man who sells in the temple, especially if he sells doves, that is, sells what the Holy Spirit reveals to him for material gain, know that by selling the work of the Holy Spirit, he is expelled from the altar of the Lord.[75]

True leadership: It often happens that those who deal with an unbalanced style and are controlled by worldly matters occupy a prominent place like a priest or sit on the seat of teaching; while those who possess spirituality and liberation from earthly matters rule over everything and are not judged by anyone, only holding a low position in the priesthood or being excluded from the general public.[76] **This abnormal situation in Origen's opinion is only super-**

---

73   *Comm. on Matt. 15:37 (Drewery).*
74   *Comm. on Matt. 16:17.*
75   *In Luc. hom. 38:5*
76   *In Numb. hom. 2:1 Church History 50 (1981) : The Charismatic Intellectual: Origen's Understanding of Religious Leadership, p. 118.*

ficial, as in the inner depths they are the elite spiritual members. Those who possess the qualities listed by Paul for those suitable for the episcopate are bishops before God, even if they are not bishops before people, as they did not reach this position through human appointment.[77]

The priesthood and internal corruption: Moses clothed Aaron, the chief priest, with garments (Numbers 8:7). It is truly said that God made them. "The Lord God made garments of skin for Adam and his wife and clothed them" (Genesis 3:21). These garments were made of animal skin, so such garments must be worn by the sinner.[78] I think that if a person claims to be a priest of God and does not have the chosen chest (or heart) among all his members, then he is not a priest. This is the leg for the priest (Numbers 7:33), which the children of Israel bring to him for their salvation.[79]

I think that the performance of the priests in their duties is one thing, and their teaching and training in everything is another. Anyone can complete religious service, but few adorn themselves with ethics, educate themselves with teaching, learn wisdom, adapt to proclaiming the truth of matters and explaining the wisdom of faith, without neglecting the ornament of understanding, and the nobility of defending the truth represented in the "golden head covering" placed on their head. Therefore, the title of the priest is one thing, and his dignity according to the merits of his life and the virtues of his soul is another.[80]

The priesthood and dwelling in the house of God: The priest does not leave the house of God, meaning that he loves heavenly life. If a person desires to become a high priest, not just in name but in merit, let him follow Moses and imitate Aaron. What was said about them? They did not leave the tent of the Lord (Numbers

---

77 Series Comm. on Matt. 12 Church History 50 (1981): The Charismatic Intellectual: Origen's Understanding of Religious Leadership.
78 Homilies on Leviticus 6:2. (See Frs. of the Church)
79 Homilies on Leviticus 5:12. (See Frs. of the Church)
80 Homilies on Leviticus 6:6. (See Frs. of the Church)

10). **Moses was in the tent of the Lord all the time.**[81] **What was his work? Either to learn something from the Lord or to teach the people. It is logical for the servants of the church and its priesthood to accept the sins of the people... as well as to strive for perfection and knowledge in the priestly duties, qualifying them to remove the sins of the people in a sacred place, in the courtyard of the tent of testimony, rather than practicing sins.**[82]

The priesthood and the life of prayer: The priest is a man of prayer, helping his people with his prayers to defeat their unseen enemies. [Would that the priest of the church pray constantly so that his people under his care may overcome the forces of the unseen Amalekites, who are the demons attacking those who seek a life of piety in Christ.][83]

The fatherhood of the priest: Origen emphasizes that priests are fatherly doctors who care for their sick children and make every effort to heal them. [Priests and teachers in the church can beget children, as is the case with the statement: "My little children, for whom I am again in the anguish of childbirth until Christ is formed in you" (Galatians 4:19); and elsewhere he also says: "For though you have countless guides in Christ, you do not have many fathers. For I became your father in Christ Jesus through the gospel" (1 Corinthians 4:15).][84]

God allows priests to feel weakness so that they may become merciful towards the weak. By recognizing their own personal sins, their dealings with sinners become more respectful in order to attract them to repentance. [But what is admirable in such a priest is not that he does not sin; this is impossible, but that he acknowledges his personal sin and feels it. Whoever thinks he does not sin does not improve his

---

81 *Homilies on Leviticus 6:6. (See Frs. of the Church)*
82 *Homilies on Leviticus 5:3. (See Frs. of the Church)*
83 *Homilies on Leviticus 6:6. (See Frs. of the Church)*
84 *Homilies on Leviticus 6:6. (See Frs. of the Church)*

own condition. And whoever is troubled by his weaknesses can more easily forgive those who sin.]⁸⁵

The priest and the spirit of leadership: One of the tasks of leaders is to create a spirit of leadership in others so that service is not concentrated only in them. [Note that the Lord addressed Moses in this matter, saying: "Pass on before the people, taking with you some of the elders of Israel" (Exodus 17:5). Moses did not lead the people to the water of the rock alone, but he had with him the elders of the people. And the law did not announce Christ alone, but the prophets, the fathers, and the elders also proclaimed Him.]⁸⁶

The priesthood and the grace of God: Divine grace prepares the prophets, messengers, evangelists, pastors, and teachers for this divine calling, and works through them.⁸⁷ If one neglects it, they fall from their calling. The care of the servants in the church is understood through failure unless Christ shepherds with them. In order to be a "teacher," this is a free grace according to the gift of Christ, so it is clear that the shepherd who shepherds his flock wisely needs a free grace that works in him...⁸⁸ [The proper tasks of the priest are of a dual nature. They are to learn from God through constant reading and meditation on the Holy Scriptures, and to teach the people. It is necessary to teach what one has learned from God, not from their own self (Ezekiel 13:2), nor through human understanding, but what the Holy Spirit guides them to. Thus, as we meditate on the stories of the Old Covenant, we remember them day and night, and we pray continually to God to reveal to us the true knowledge of what we read, and to show us how to keep the spiritual law in our understanding and in our actions. Let us

---

85 *In Lev. hom. 2:3 (cf. G.W. Barkley - Frs. of the Church).*
86 *In Exodus hom. 11:2 (Cf. Ronad E Heine- Frs. of the Church, vol. 71.)*
87 *In Luc. hom. 12:2.*
88 *Comm. on Eph. 17 on 4:11 ff.*

qualify for the spiritual grace and be enlightened by the law of the Holy Spirit.][89]

The general priesthood: Origen refers in his sermons to the general priesthood of all members of the church. He says: [Do you want to know the difference between the priesthood of God and the priesthood of Pharaoh? Pharaoh granted priesthood based on land, but God says to His priesthood: "I am your portion." Have you not noticed, O readers, that all of you are priests of the Lord... Let us listen to what our Lord Jesus Christ commands as His priesthood: "Whoever does not renounce all that he has cannot be My disciple" (Luke 14:21). I shudder when I pronounce these words, for above all, I blame and condemn myself. If Christ refuses to count those who have anything and do not renounce all their possessions, what are we doing? How can we read and interpret that for the people, we who not only keep what we have but also desire to acquire what we did not have before coming to Christ? If our conscience accuses us, can we deceive it in what is written? I do not want to increase my sense of guilt.][90]

[Did you know that the priesthood (general) has been given to you, I mean to the whole church of God and to the people of believers?! Listen to Peter as he says to the believers: "But you are a chosen race, a royal priesthood, a holy nation, a people for His own possession" (1 Peter 2:9). Therefore, you have the priesthood as you are a priestly race, you are required to offer the sacrifice of praise (Hebrews 13:15) and the sacrifice of prayers, the sacrifice of mercy, the sacrifice of purity, and the sacrifice of holiness.][91]

---

89 *In Lev. hom.* 6:6.
90 *In Gen. hom.* 16:5.
91 *Homilies on Leviticus 9:1;* Thomas Halton, p. 146.

What is the mystery of the arrangement of the sacrifices offered by the general priesthood?

1. Sacrifice of Praise: All believers, whether from the priesthood or the laity, are required to offer the sacrifice of praise, giving it priority over the rest of the sacrifices specific to the general priesthood. The ultimate goal of faith is for all members of the church to enjoy glorified membership in the bride church, and to declare their joy in the heavenly bridegroom Christ, the Lord of glory Jesus, alongside the Father's authority over them, and the fiery work of the Holy Spirit in their hearts. A true believer does not know despair or anxiety, but enjoys a foretaste of heaven, singing with the Apostle Paul: "And raised us up with him and seated us with him in the heavenly places in Christ Jesus" (Ephesians 2:6).

2. **Sacrifice of Prayers: Believers practice prayers whether in the church, at home, or at work... not as a routine but with a fiery spiritual zeal, never ceasing to speak with their Father God openly and secretly. What they seek is to enjoy the kingdom of God within them, repeating: "Come, Lord Jesus" (Revelation 22:20).**

3. Sacrifice of Mercy: "Be merciful, just as your Father is merciful" (Luke 6:36). "Judgment without mercy will be shown to anyone who has not been merciful. Mercy triumphs over judgment" (James 2:13).

4. Sacrifice of Purity: "The goal of this command is love, which comes from a pure heart and a good conscience and a sincere faith" (1 Timothy 1:5). "Keeping a clear conscience, so that those who speak maliciously against your good behavior in Christ may be ashamed of their slander" (1 Peter 3:2).

5. Sacrifice of Holiness: "But just as he who called you is holy, so

be holy in all you do; for it is written: 'Be holy, because I am holy'" (1 Peter 1:15-16).

Most of us dedicate most of our time to the matters of this life, devoting only a little time and effort to God. In this, we resemble the members of the tribes who had little interaction with the priests, performing their religious duties in the shortest possible time. As for those who dedicate themselves to the divine word, having nothing to occupy them except the service of God, it is not unnatural to invite them to be Levites and priests due to the difference in work between the two situations. Those who perform more distinguished tasks than their brethren may be considered as chief priests akin to the rank of Aaron.[92]

The Democracy of the Church

Origen says: "Anyone called to the episcopate is not called to rule, but to serve the church." As part of the priesthood, you must offer the gift of prayer, mercy, purity, and holiness.[93]

R. Cadieu says that these historians told us that the oldest thing mentioned in the works of Saint Jerome is that the bishop of Alexandria since the early ages of the church was chosen from among the members of the clergy of Alexandria. He was selected and appointed by the clergy, in a manner similar to the emperor being chosen by the army. As we were told, this primitive custom was ended by the successors of Patriarch Demetrius. With the beginning of the post-Demetrius era, the election of the patriarch and his consecration was done by the neighboring bishops in the traditional manner, but not by choosing from among the ranks of the Alexandrian clergy. Origen shed light on the election of bishops in his time. Ferguson used his sermons on Numbers

---

92   *In Joan. 1:3 PG 14:25; R. Cadiou: Origen, Herder Book Co., 1944, p. 310.*
93   *In Isa. hom 6 PG 13:239.*

13:4 as evidence that in the third century AD, there were at least four ways to elect bishops:[94]

1. Popular election.

2. Appointment by the ruling bishop (patriarch).

3. Approval of a certain person, or confirmation of the one elected by the people.

4. Election by the clergy for him, which Origen preferred.[95]

Origen emphasizes that the presence of the people is required in the consecration of the priest, as they are the ones who elect him.[96] [The consecration of the priest requires the presence of the people, so that everyone knows what confirms to them that the person elected for the priesthood is the most prominent among them, the most knowledgeable and holy, and the richest in every virtue.][97]

It is necessary for this to be a public decision so that no one from the people has a different opinion. This opinion is based on the fact that Moses "gathered all the congregation" (Numbers 8:3).

---

94 R. Cadiou: *Origen*, Herder Book Co., 1944, p. 317-8.
95 F. Ferguson: "*Origen and the Election of Bishops.*" Church History 43 (1974), 27-30, 32.
96 *Ep. 48 ad Amun.*
97 *SC 286, 279; Thomas Halton, p. 21*

20

ORIGEN AND MARTYRDOM

Origen longed in his youth to be martyred with his father Leonidas, and martyrdom was the cornerstone of his education. When he took over the leadership of the school of Alexandria, he courageously supported many of his students who were martyred and stood by them until the last moments. He considered that he was called to the mission of preparing Christians for martyrdom. He also prepared the hearts of the catechumens to face martyrdom with joy. He missed them in their captivity, defended them, and gave them fraternal kisses openly in the halls of the courts.

When Origen advanced in age, he recorded his feelings about the persecution that had swept through Alexandria forty years earlier. In his "Homilies on Jeremiah," he described the persecuted Church of Alexandria, saying: [This happened when the Christian was a true believer who courageously went to the church to be martyred. We would usually return from the tombs, where we were in the company of the bodies of the saints, to our meetings held in the steadfast church. The catechumens listened to the sermons in an atmosphere filled with love for martyrdom; they overcame the pain, confessed the living God without fear. We saw truly miraculous heroic deeds. The believers were few in number, but they believed in the truth; and they made progress on the straight and narrow path that leads to life.]

During the persecution of Maximianus, Origen wrote: "Encouragement for martyrdom." This work carried the same message as his letter to his father when he was a boy, elaborating in accordance with his maturity. He wrote it in Caesarea Palestine in 235 AD, and addressed it to Ambrosius and Bertucutius, priests of Caesarea, who were imprisoned, and he declared martyrdom as his sweet desire sought by his soul.

Origen stood alongside Saint Ignatius of Antioch in his desire for martyrdom. He also stood with Saint Clemens of Alexandria who taught that martyrdom is the completion of love. He considered martyrdom as evidence of the truth of Christianity, not just to show the ability of Christians to die for their faith, as there are others who also die for their love of their country and principles, but because the contempt for death among Christian martyrs indicates that they have broken the forces of evil that used death as a tool for torture (1 Cor 15:55). Martyrdom highlighted the power of the resurrection as a living reality, with the appearance of the miraculous deeds of the martyrs, especially their rise above pain. In addition to its great historical value, as a primary source on the persecution of Maximianus, it is considered an important document that reveals the hope of Egyptian Christians in the first half of the third century.

Contents of the article

This article can be divided into five parts:

1. **Encouragement for martyrdom: Origen, like Ambrosius, said: "The need for martyrdom has become urgent." Martyrdom is the holiest task of the Christian human, through it he shows his longing for union with God. He believed that martyrs receive a special beatification more than all the saints. They are chosen**

by God, they sit beside Him on the throne of judgment, and through their blood, they have the power to achieve forgiveness of sins for others.

Origen wonders: What greater joy is there than the joy of martyrdom? Where many crowds gather to witness the final hours of the martyr. Let each of us remember how many times we have been exposed to the danger of ordinary death, then we ask ourselves whether God has preserved us for what is better; preserved us for the baptism of blood that washes our sins, and allows us to take our place in the heavenly altar with our companions in spiritual jihad. Let faith and courage be with you, prepare yourselves to achieve the blessedness of martyrdom. "We are the children of the patient God and the brothers of the patient Christ; let us then show ourselves patient in all that befalls us." And the best that befalls us is death as martyrs.

* Perseverance and steadfastness in trials, because after a brief pain we attain our eternal rewards (vv. 1-2).

* Martyrdom is a duty for the true Christian, because whoever loves God desires union with Him (vv. 3-4).

* Only those who confess faith courageously can enter into eternal happiness (v. 5).

2. **Warning against apostasy and idol worship:**

    * Denying the true God and worshiping false gods is the greatest of sins (v. 6), for it is foolish to worship the creature instead of the Creator (v. 7). God intends to save souls from idol worship (vv. 8-9).

    * Those who practice this sin enter into union with idols and receive their punishment after death (v. 10).

3. **Bearing the cross with perseverance alongside Christ:**

- By truly seeking martyrdom. Salvation is attained by bearing one's cross with Christ (vv. 11-13).

- The reward will be greater if compared to the worldly possessions left behind (vv. 14-16).

- Denouncing pagan idols and joining the ranks of confessors does not allow us to break our covenants (v. 17).

- The conduct of martyrs is judged by the whole world (v. 18).

- We must accept all forms of martyrdom so that we are not counted among the fallen angels (vv. 19-20).

4. **Biblical examples of perseverance and endurance:**

    - The Second Book of Maccabees presents the story of Eleazar and the seven sons of the courageous mother (vv. 22-27).

5. **The necessity of martyrdom, its essence, and types:**

    - It is fitting for Christians to endure this death, to repay to God the blessings He has bestowed upon them (vv. 28-29).

    - The serious sins committed after baptism by water can only be forgiven by baptism of blood (v. 30).

The souls of those who resist the temptation of the wicked (v. 32) and dedicate their lives to the Lord as a pure sacrifice do not only enter eternal bliss (v. 31), but are granted forgiveness of sins by those who pray for them (v. 30).

Just as the hand of God reached out to help the three young men in the fiery furnace, and Daniel in the lion's den, so the martyrs will not be deprived of His support (v. 33).

The Father desires this sacrifice and so does Christ, for if we deny Him, He will deny us in heaven (v. 34-35).

Faith leads the confessors to paradise, for those who despise the world will inherit the kingdom (v. 36-39).

His children who are left behind on earth will be showered with His blessings (v. 38).

Whoever denies the Son denies the Father. And if we follow the example of Christ and offer our lives for the kingdom, we will enjoy His consolation (v. 40-42). Therefore, Christians are called to be prepared for martyrdom (v. 43-44).

Verses 45 and 46 address a side issue, which is not venerating the devil, as the name we invoke is God, and the final part of the article emphasizes perseverance and courage (v. 47-49).

Martyrdom in Origen and Saint Ignatius

Saint Ignatius criticizes those who provoke rulers, officials, and soldiers recklessly, seeking persecution. He explains that a true Christian does not fear death, but it is not right for him to seek it hastily. This is considered a form of suicide against God's will, resembling the Indian ascetics who throw themselves into fire. Martyrdom for Saint Ignatius is a daily test and a good testimony to Christ through words, actions, and the entire life of a Christian. Origen, on the other hand, urges believers to strive for martyrdom as a precious opportunity for the soul to gain freedom and for the Church to gain glory. Origen constantly desired martyrdom, explaining in his article "Encouragement to Martyrdom" and in his sermons the appreciation he held for this ultimate testimony of our belonging to Christ, while also avoiding extremism on the matter.

Martyrdom in Origen and the theologian Tertullian

Origen and Tertullian both encourage believers to martyrdom, each with their own perspective.

Gregory Dix sees Tertullian focusing on the resurrection of the body and its salvation from eternal punishment, while Origen focuses on the liberation and growth of the soul, through its learning by the Logos, so that it may enjoy resurrection with Him. Tertullian views martyrdom as a means to glorify our resurrected body, while Origen sees it as a royal path, through which Jesus Christ the Logos and teacher of the soul enters with it into the embrace of the Father, revealing to it the divine mysteries. For Origen, the revelation of mysteries, or attaining true knowledge of God, is the true eternal glory for the soul that becomes in companionship with the heavenly Father. Origen says: "Then, as friends, you will know the Father and the heavenly Teacher, for you have not known Him face to face (1 Cor 13:12). Friends do not learn through riddles, but through what can be seen, or through wisdom abstracted from words, symbols, and forms. It will be possible to achieve this, by reaching the nature of the things perceived, and the beauty of truth. If you believe that Paul was caught up to the third heaven and to paradise, where he heard words that cannot be expressed, which is not lawful for a man to utter (2 Cor 12:2, 4), then you will realize that you will know things greater than what was revealed to Paul and that descended from the third heaven. As for you, you will not descend if you carry the cross and follow Jesus, the chief priest who passed through the heavens (Heb 4:14). If you do not turn away from following Him, you will ascend through the heavens, not only above the earth and its mysteries, but also above the heavens and their mysteries."

Origen's longing for martyrdom

It seems that martyrdom in Origen's view is a means to achieve complete purity, which even personal holiness cannot provide. It is the final preparation for the truth in standing at the heavenly altar. This was the image of martyrdom that he wanted every Christian to achieve. He always said that the Church without martyrs would be deserted and desolate, like Jerusalem without sacrifices offered in the temple.

Meanings of martyrdom

1. Origen believes that Christ Himself, the Lord of martyrs, is the true martyr who works in the lives of those who believe in Him. He endured many persecutions, and declared that Christ allows pains for the martyr as He suffers in His martyrs. He grants them victory, crowns them with the laurel, and accepts that laurel in Himself. He realizes that the absolute loyalty of the Christian martyr carries within it a convincing power capable of making the pagans see the truth.

2. Martyrdom is the task of every true Christian who longs for union with God, and striving for His righteousness.

3. [I urge you to remember amidst your temporal struggles the great reward prepared in heaven for the persecuted and reviled for righteousness' sake. Rejoice and be glad, for great is your reward in heaven (Matt 5:10-12), as the apostles did when they were counted worthy to suffer shame for His name (Acts 5:41). If you feel yourself on the verge of despair, let "the mind that is in Christ" (Phil 2:5) address it: "Why are you cast down, O my soul? And why are you disquieted within me? Hope in God, for I shall yet praise Him" (Psalm 42:11).] [Just as "he who is joined to a harlot is one body with her" (1 Cor 6:16), so is he who confesses a god, especially when tested in his faith, he is mingled with the god he confesses and united with him. If he denies him, his denial is a sword that cuts him off from the one he denied, suffering amputation as he separates himself from the one he denied.]

4. The martyrs are the beloved of God, who express their love for Him by sacrificing even their temporary lives.

5. Martyrdom is necessary for our salvation. It is sharing with Christ in His crucifixion, and practicing the Gospel life. [Among our covenants with God, the comprehensive citizenship of the Gospel,

the Gospel becomes our homeland where we submit to its laws, which say: "If anyone desires to come after Me, let him deny himself, and take up his cross, and follow Me. For whoever desires to save his life will lose it, but whoever loses his life for My sake will find it" (Matt 16:24-25).

6. True Christians may endure persecution for Christ, responding to His love practically with their love for Him. [We can learn from this what martyrdom means, and how it leads to strong trust in God. The saint is characterized by generosity, desiring to respond to what God has bestowed upon him with blessings, searching for what he can do for God in return for every gift, finding nothing that balances these blessings more than martyrdom.]

7. Martyrdom is a precious death granted to the chosen by our Savior. [It is clear that the "cup of salvation" mentioned in the Psalms (Psalm 116:13) is the death of martyrs... The precious death will come to us if we are the righteous of the Lord, deserving of death... It is a Christian, powerful, and holy death.]

8. Through martyrdom, we become brothers to the apostles. [The exhortation to martyrdom mentioned in the Gospel of Matthew was directed only to "the twelve," and it is fitting for us to heed it as well, thereby becoming brothers to the apostles and part of them.]

9. Martyrdom is a baptism of blood and a source of forgiveness for sins. The virtue of the martyr's death extends to many.

10. [We have preserved for the baptism of blood that washes our sins, and allows us to take our place at the heavenly altar.]

11. Martyrdom is the path to eternal glory. [God spoke to Abraham one day, saying, "Go from your land." Perhaps we also hear Him in the near future addressing us, saying, "Go from every land." We do well if we obey Him, so that we may behold the place called "the kingdom of heaven."]

12. In his article "Encouragement to Martyrdom," Origen says that the believer in martyrdom can offer himself, as a true priest and sacrifice to God. Just as Jesus redeemed us with His precious blood, so can the martyr's precious blood save others. Martyrdom is a "golden work" and "cup of salvation." The martyr offers all his wealth, family, and children.

13. The early Christians believed that Christ's victory over death on the cross shattered Satan's most powerful weapons, namely the fear of death. Origen sees the martyr joining Christ in His war against the devil and his forces. The martyr is a wrestler, and his martyrdom is a battle fought in a arena with demonic forces, trying to push him to offer sacrifices to idols, until they regain their power through his defeat. At the same time, heavenly witnesses surround him, waiting for his victory over the principalities and forces in the world of demons. The martyr is considered especially as a complement to what Christ had accomplished, as He became the Lord over death and Satan, and gave humanity its freedom. [We must consider that the blood of the holy martyrs has liberated us from harmful forces. For example, their steadfastness and endurance, their confession unto death, their zeal for religion, and their resistance to evil forces' conspiracies against humanity in its suffering, this is the kind of service offered by the deaths of the righteous martyrs.]

14. Martyrdom for Origen is the Christian's test of preferring spiritual things over physical ones. [He believed that they love God with all their souls. And out of their desire to be united with Him, they withdraw and separate themselves, not only from the earthly body, but also from all worldly matters that could distance them from God. Like these, they are willing to lay down their humble bodies, without sorrow or emotion, when the time comes to shed the body of death, which is generally seen as death.]

15. The best rational sacrifices are martyrdom, then virginity, and staying away from pride, greed, and lies...

In his commentary on the Book of Psalms, he wrote that it is our duty to offer a sacrifice of denying our own wisdom, as this is a form of martyrdom. [Inside each of us is a mind that we must break, with the intention of turning it into a sacrifice for God.]

Martyrdom and Preaching the Gospel

Martyrs give their testimony before unbelievers and bear witness to the true light.

Martyrs encourage witnessing for Christ without fear. Christians return from the graves after carrying the bodies of the holy martyrs, gather in the church for prayer, show signs of holiness and fearlessness.

Reward of Martyrdom

First: The martyr carries his cross with Christ, leaving his life so that Christ may live in him. He follows Christ in His sufferings, then in His glory, as He sits at the right hand of the Father. Participation in suffering leads to participation in victory. His reward is to be united with Christ forever and glorified with Him. The reward of martyrdom, as all Christians believe, is a joy that cannot be expressed, but for Origen, it is a distinct intellectual joy. [Each of our members has a specific ability that corresponds to its nature. The eyes see visible things, the ears hear sounds, so the mind is specialized in perceptible things and in God who transcends them. So why hesitate and doubt in removing the corruptible bodies that hinder and weigh down our souls?... where we enjoy with Jesus Christ the rest that accompanies beatitude, and contemplate the living Word, in its completeness, when we feed on it, and realize His comprehensive wisdom, and our minds are enlightened by the light of true knowledge that never fades.] [This leads us to believe

that the death of the holy martyrs defeats the forces of evil. As if their patience, confession until death, and zeal for piety alleviate the severity of attacks by evil forces against the afflicted. And as a result of the enemy's stagnation and exhaustion in their forces, many of those who were defeated by them raise their heads, liberated from the weight of the forces of evil under which they had fallen and were harmed.]

[We must assume that many benefit beyond description from the death of the holy martyrs.]

Second: Origen sees martyrdom as the joy of the Christian. He says: "We are only persecuted if God allows the persecutor and gives him the authority to persecute us. So if His will is for us to continue the struggle and jihad for our faith, we say, "I can do all things through Christ who strengthens me."

Thirdly: Origen repeats his statement that God does not judge the martyrs, but they sit with Him in judgment. [Martyrdom is called a cup, as is evident from the words: "Father, if it is possible, let this cup pass from me; yet not my will, but yours be done." We also learn that whoever drinks from the cup that Jesus drank from, sits beside the King of kings, judging and condemning.]

Fourthly: Since the martyrs are sacrifices offered by the Church, we obtain forgiveness of sins through their intercession. The sacrifices of the Church are connected to the unique sacrifice of the Lord Christ. They offered their lives as a sacrifice of love, extending its effectiveness to others [In this way, we must assume the value of the deaths of the holy martyrs, through which many benefit beyond description.] Francis Young says: The idea that the martyr's sacrifice has an expiatory nature has not completely disappeared, and it is closely related to the death of the great Christ, who atoned for the sins of the whole world. In fact, the Jewish tradition of martyrdom may have provided the oldest means of interpreting the death of Christ. However, considering that the death of Christ

on the cross is the only sacrifice for the sins of the whole world, it is difficult to justify this insistence on the expiation of Christian martyrdom, unless we assume that this doctrine entered Christian thought independently. The problem of obtaining forgiveness of sins following baptism must have reinforced the idea of the possibility of washing away human sins through the baptism of blood. The martyr's death is not limited to atoning for the sins of the perpetrators, but extends to many with our companions in the spiritual struggle.

[Let us remember our sins, and that it is impossible to obtain forgiveness without baptism (see Acts 2:38). And according to the Gospel commandments, one cannot be baptized again with water and the Spirit for the forgiveness of sins, so the only option left is baptism of blood through martyrdom.]

Those who served at the altar established by the law of Moses were assumed to intercede for the forgiveness of sins for the people, through the blood of goats and bulls, just as the souls of those who "were beheaded for their testimony to Jesus" (Rev 20:4) do not serve in vain at the heavenly altar, but obtain forgiveness for their sins through those who pray for them. We also learn that just as Jesus Christ, the great high priest, offered himself as a sacrifice, so do the priests offer themselves as sacrifices (Heb 5, 7, 8, 10). Therefore, they are seen in their rightful place at the altar. However, while some priests were without fault and offered blameless sacrifices in their divine service, others among them were full of flaws as outlined by Moses in the book of Leviticus (21:17 ff), leading to their exclusion from the altar. So who then is the priest without fault, if not the one who confessed until the end, and possessed all that we mean by martyrdom.

The Arena of Conflict: In Origen's commentary on the fall of the walls of Jericho, he says: [Let us go to war to attack one of the most dangerous cities in the world, I mean evil. Let us bring down the towering walls of sin. The battle you are engaged in is within

you, so there is the structure of evil that needs to be destroyed. Drive your enemy out of your heart!]

Martyrdom and Sacrifice: Martyrdom and sacrifice are one and the same. If a Christian fails to train himself to consider human life as a whole as a test that requires him to muster all his courage, he will find himself at risk of relapse during the trial. Origen realized that the "burnt offering" in the Old Testament meant the highest offering "of praise". Therefore, his treatment of the Christian burnt offering included the same idea. The Christian's burnt offering is "himself", which he keeps burning on the altar by abandoning his possessions, carrying his cross, following Christ by offering his body to burn, and following the glory of the martyr, with his love for his brothers, and striving for truth and justice, until the world crucifies him, and he is for the world.

Martyrdom as a "Defeat of the Devils": Francis Young says: We must look at the martyrdom as a sacrifice of love for God, and a victory over the devils. It is not surprising to find that the death of the Lord of the martyrs, Jesus Christ, as a sacrifice is used as a means to drive away the evil demons.

Origen urges his readers to persevere in the war against the demons, insisting that idol worship is the only alternative to martyrdom. He explains that the rewards of martyrdom are the realization that humans do not err and the enjoyment of heavenly bliss. He also describes the atoning value of the martyr's sacrifice, presenting the joy of sharing in Christ's sufferings and emulating him. The martyr's work in Christ is to strip away evil principalities and powers, and to triumph over them, by sharing in Christ's sufferings... For Origen, the martyr's sacrifice is offered as a ransom to ward off the rule of evil, as part of the war against the devil.

21

ORIGEN AND CHRISTIAN WORSHIP

Worship and Reaching the Eternal Inheritance?

Origen says, "True repentance is to read the old books (i.e. the books of the Old Testament), and to know who the righteous are and emulate them, and who the sinners are and avoid falling into their mistakes; and to read the books of the New Testament and the words of the apostles. After reading, we write everything we have read in our hearts and apply it in our lives so that we are not given a book of divorce, but we can attain the eternal inheritance, and when the nations are saved, Israel also will be able to be saved. 'For I do not want you, brethren, to be uninformed of this mystery—so that you will not be wise in your own estimation—that a partial hardening has happened to Israel until the fullness of the Gentiles has come in; and so all Israel will be saved' (Romans 11:25-26), 'and they will be one flock with one shepherd.'"[1]

---

1 Origen, Homilies on Jeremiah, Homily 4 (translated by Jacqueline Samir Kosti),

What is the desired worship?

Origen says:

"Extended prayer and abundant tears attract God's mercy."

"Only through weeping can one attain the desired joy."

"Jesus wanted to demonstrate in himself all the beatitudes, as he said, 'Blessed are those who mourn,' and he himself wept in order to establish this beatitude well."[2]

What are the rituals of desired worship?

1. The orientation towards the east during prayer: In the fifth sermon on the Book of Numbers, Origen hints at the customs of Christians. Often, we prostrate ourselves to pray and turn towards the east, as our eyes must remain fixed with our hearts towards the rising of the true light. What is astonishing in this book is that it shows that this tradition is not exclusive to public prayer alone, but also to private prayer. As for the importance of the symbolism of this tradition, Origen says that it was practiced because Christ is the new sun of the universe, that is, the Church.

    Circumstances may compel us to pray in a different direction if we are forced to pray while sitting and both feet are sick, or if we are feverish, or if we are lying down.

2. As for prayer while we are prostrating, what you need to know is that it is necessary to acknowledge our sins to the Lord, seek His forgiveness, and return to the right position. The symbol of prostration and submission is what Paul speaks of when he says, "For this reason I bow my knees before the Father, from whom every family in heaven and on earth is named" (Ephesians 3:14). This spiritual bowing is also called because all holy rational creatures

---

2 In Jer. hom 3:49; In Luc. hom 18.

worship the Lord and submit before Him. When you hear the name Jesus, it means what the apostle thinks when he says, "so that at the name of Jesus every knee should bow, in heaven and on earth and under the earth" (Philippians 2:10).

3. Stretching out our hands and lifting our eyes: The preferred position is undoubtedly stretching out our hands and lifting our eyes, which is the best expression of our attitude during prayer. He says that we should stretch ourselves before stretching out our hands, and lift our minds to the Lord before lifting our eyes to Him. And before we stand, we must empty our minds of all preoccupation with earthly matters and place them before the Lord of the universe. We must also set aside any resentment when we feel wronged, if we desire the Lord to forgive us for the mistakes we have made.

4. The special place for prayer: Any place that is suitable for prayer if you pray well in it. And if you want to pray quietly and without distraction, you should choose a special place in your home, if you have a sacred place where you pray. The special grace and benefit come from the place of prayer, and by that I mean the place where believers gather, because it is reasonable to assume that angelic forces are present when believers gather together, and that the influence of the Lord Savior is also there, as well as the spirits of the saints who are still alive, although it is not easy to say that.

And when you look at the Savior now with your eyes, in this gathering and in this church, and when the most spiritual part of your eyes looks, they both look at Jesus. "Blessed are your eyes for they see" (Matt 13:16). This gathering also befits baptized Christians, men, women, and children, as they look at our Lord Jesus, not only with their physical eyes, but with their souls as well. When you look at Him through His grace with contemplation, your faces shine with a clearer light, and you can say, "You have put gladness in my heart" (Psalm 4:7).

What is the concept of fasting?

Origen speaks about fasting, which is the abstention from food that the people participate in, according to the Christian system. He says that we should fast on the fourth and sixth days of the week, which are Wednesday and Friday. And of course, there is freedom for the Christian person to fast at any time, not as an excessive obligation, but with moderation.

The meaning of fasting: Do you still want me to show you the appropriate type of fasting for you? Fast from every sin, do not take the food of hatred, do not take the fasting of pain, do not burn with the wine of luxury. Fast from evil deeds, stay away from wicked words, guard yourself from evil thoughts. Do not touch the secrets of deviant teachings. Do not desire the deceitful food of philosophy that misleads you from the truth. This fasting pleases the Lord. But "abstain from the food which God created, to be received with thanksgiving by those who believe" (1 Tim 4:3)... When the Pharisees were angry with the Lord because His disciples were not fasting, He replied to them, saying, "Can the friends of the bridegroom mourn as long as the bridegroom is with them? But the days will come when the bridegroom will be taken away from them, and then they will fast" (Matt 9:15). Therefore, let them fast when the bridegroom is not with them, but those who have the bridegroom with them should not fast.

What is the concept of the Lord's Day?

The blessed person is the one who listens to the words of the Lord and his deeds and thoughts. That is why he lives in the days of the Lord continuously, and all his days become the days of the Lord.

How do we preach the Gospel?

The priest must watch his preaching to be without fault and his instructions to be without errors, but with perfection. This means that if we can present ourselves first, and make our members dead to sin, so that not only in teachings, but also in our lives we make sure that our sacrifice is accepted by the Lord, and we gain the salvation of those who hear it. Preaching the Gospel is a type of worship and offering. No one offers it to the Lord unless he is sound and aware of his salvation, offering it with thanksgiving to the Lord.

The person must watch his preaching to be without fault, and his instructions to be without errors, offering them with majestic perfection. This means that if possible, we present ourselves first, and make our members dead to sin... And no one offers this offering to the Lord unless he is sound and aware of his salvation, and offers his thanks to the Lord. Therefore, any spiritually sick and weak person cannot offer a "beneficial offering".

How do women offer their prayers?

I do not hesitate to say that the angels are present among our people. And if we say anything still in the word, they rejoice and pray with us. And because the angels are present in the church, which is the church of Christ, then women are asked to cover their heads and men to bow in reverence.

The concept of worship

Worship means the complete submission of a person with love to God working in him, internally and externally, while rejecting false worship such as idol worship. It says, "The Lord made a covenant with them and commanded them, saying: Do not fear other gods, nor bow down to them, nor worship them, nor sacrifice to them" (2 Kings 17:35).

Sometimes some people worship even against their will, such as flattery to kings when they see their passion in this type.

Worship and rituals

There are rituals within the practices of the church that everyone must perform, and yet not everyone understands the meaning behind this ritual. For example, we bow down to pray, and we face the east while praying.

23

THE SIGN OF ORIGEN AND THE HOLY EUCHARIST

The Holy Eucharist, the body of Christ.

Origen said to Celsus, "We eat bread through the virtue of prayer, it becomes a body, and it purifies those who use it deeply... The Holy Eucharist is classified as the same word. And in Contra Celsus, Origen wrote, "We give thanks to the Creator of all, and with thanks and prayer for the blessing we have received, we also eat the bread that is presented to us, and this bread becomes a holy body through prayer, which purifies those who take it."

Origen sees in his sermon on Saint John, "The unworthy one who eats the bread of the Lord and drinks his cup, eats and drinks according to his deeds, the effect of good things in a righteous soul, and evil things in their evil. The morsel that Christ gave (to Judas) is of the same kind, which the other apostles gave, saying, "Take and eat," and it was for their salvation, and it was for the condemnation of Judas, so that after the morsel, Satan entered into him.

The connection between the Holy Eucharist and the Holy Scripture.

This bread, which is the body of the Lord, the word that nourishes the soul, and the word that comes from the Lord, the word, and the bread from the heavenly bread that is placed on the table, and the word that satisfies and rejoices the hearts of those who drink from it, and drink it in that cup... And as mentioned earlier, in the form of the baptism that was in the cloud and the sea, but now the renewal is in the water and the Holy Spirit. And as the manna was food, but now it reveals the word of the Lord as true food, as he himself said, "For my flesh is true food, and my blood is true drink."

What does it mean to approach such great rituals? Christ enters as food through the leadership of the saints of the Church, whom the Lord delights in, and when you take the body and blood of the Lord, it enters under your roof. It is said that we drink the blood of Christ, not only as a mystery, but also take His words that make up life, as He says, "The words that I speak to you are spirit, and they are life" (John 6:63). Origen clearly believes that he took the Holy Eucharist, the word of the Lord, which enlightens the ignorance of the world. The Eucharist gives understanding as well as discernment, and the meal unites the Church with the risen Christ.

The worthiness of receiving the Holy Eucharist

The fact that the Holy Eucharist can be eaten to condemnation, a fact demonstrated by the Last Supper.

This dinner was for the salvation of all the disciples except for Judas, who was condemned. Origen interpreted this to mean that the word that brings salvation to the soul, which is originally true, can be a source of the worst evil if given to a sick (spiritually) self. It is stated in Matthew 26:23, "He who dips his hand with Me in the dish will betray Me." Origen explains that those who take communion while harboring ill feelings towards their brothers imitate Judas the betrayer. This also applies to anyone in the church who conspires against their brothers and partakes of the same table of Christ's body and the same cup containing His blood.

23

THE SIGNIFICANCE OF ORIGEN AND BAPTISM

Origen praises baptism as a new birth, a participation in the divine nature, an acceptance of bodily membership in the Church, a return to paradise, and an acceptance of the general priesthood.

Baptism is the essential first step in the journey to the Lord. It purifies, begets, and presents the person to Christ, and bestows the Holy Spirit.

The Baptism of Jesus

For Origen, the focus is directly on the baptism of Christ Himself. What happened in the Jordan River also happens in the baptismal font.

Preparation for Baptism.

You also, as you desire to receive the Holy Sacrament and the grace of the Holy Spirit, must first purify yourself by hearing the word of the Lord. You must restrain the evils of the barbaric and savage nature by cultivating calmness and humility, then you can receive the grace of the Holy Spirit.

Not everyone is "baptized into salvation". Those who have received the grace of baptism in the name of Christ have been "baptized", but I cannot say that everyone has been baptized for salvation. Simon was "baptized", but because he was not baptized for salvation, he was cursed by the one who said to him, "May your silver perish with you" (Acts 8:20). It is difficult for one who is baptized to be baptized for salvation. Listen to him and prepare yourselves while you have not received anything but baptism. The one who is baptized, but not for salvation, receives the water but does not receive the Holy Spirit. But the one who is baptized for salvation receives both. The benefit of baptism depends on the intention of the one who receives it, so if he repents, he receives it.

1. Origen sees baptism as a tomb, those who are candidates for it participate in death, burial, and resurrection (Romans 6:1-11).

2. Baptism is the "new or second circumcision".

3. Baptism is the mystery of enlightenment. Blessed are those who become close to it! They become near the fire that illuminates them without burning them.

4. Baptism is the secret of the union between heaven and earth. Origen believes that the crossing of the Red Sea under the leadership of Moses was a symbol of baptism in the Old Covenant, while the crossing of the Jordan River under the leadership of Joshua was a symbol of baptism in the New Covenant. The Red Sea was divided and everyone crossed through the waters, while in the Jordan River, the waters were only on one side. This symbolizes the union of heaven and earth and the destruction of the wall that separates them.

5. Do you not believe with me that all sins, along with their kings, have been removed from us in the waters of baptism? This is what

the Apostle Paul desired to say after enumerating all types of sin. Baptism is called "the washing of generations" and is accompanied by the renewal of the spirit, which contemplates the world. When you come to Jesus and receive the grace of baptism for the forgiveness of sins, you yourself will be delivered from war, on the condition that you bear the humiliation of Jesus Christ in the body, so that the life of Jesus may be manifested in our bodies (2 Corinthians 4:10). Therefore, the war ends within you, and you become peaceful, and are called a child of the Lord (Matthew 5:9).

6. Baptism ignites the soul with the fire of the Holy Spirit.

A. Baptism frees us from the power of Satan.

B. Baptism makes us members of the Church in the body of Christ. The Holy Spirit creates in us new people and renews the face of the earth. Through the grace of the Spirit within us, He removes "the old self with its practices" (Colossians 3:9) and begins us on the journey of new life (Romans 6:4).

Baptism and Sonship to the Father

Through baptism, we receive sonship to the Father by the grace of the Holy Spirit. And from our side, we must say to the Lord "Our Father," not only with our lips but through a holy life that corresponds to our sonship to the Father.

Baptism of Blood

Let us remember the sins we have committed, which it is impossible to have forgiven apart from baptism. According to the law of the Gospel, it is impossible to repeat baptism with water and the Spirit for the forgiveness of our sins, for baptism by martyrdom has been given to us.

Baptism of Infants

The first church insisted on baptizing children, so that they may experience the grace of their salvation. For every living being is born in sin, and that is why it was an apostolic tradition to baptize newborns. Origen witnessed the baptism of children. The church followed the example of the apostles in baptizing even the little ones. Since the mysteries of divine care were entrusted to them, they knew that everyone had violations from the original sin, which needed to be washed away by water and the Spirit. And if you want to hear what other saints felt about physical birth, listen to David when he says, "Behold, I was brought forth in iniquity, and in sin did my mother conceive me" (Psalm 51:5), and he affirms that every soul is born in the flesh, stained with injustice and sin. Therefore, "there is no one who is pure, even if their life on earth is only one day" (Job 14:1-6).

Garslov Blakean says in his writings that the practice of baptizing children was derived from the apostolic origin and was preserved to become a church tradition. The grace of baptism may seem unnecessary. So why is infant baptism included in the church tradition? To answer the multiple considerations, he suggests as a preliminary answer that "children are baptized for the forgiveness of sins," what sins? When did they sin? And how can children be a reason for cleansing, unless it is based on the idea that no one is clean from impurity, not even if their life on earth is only for one day. And because the impurity of birth is removed through baptism.

Baptism and the ongoing spiritual struggle.

Origen says that the risen Christ is light. And the "power" of Christ as he rose is not only present in the believer at baptism, but also in his constant struggle in the "new life." He is now called the light of humanity, the true light, and the light of the world because he illuminates and shines upon all rational beings. Likewise, because of the power by which he sets aside old death and causes superabundant life to take its place, even those who receive him rise again from death, and this is called resurrection. He does this not only at the moment when a person says, "We were buried with Christ through baptism and rose again with him," but also when everything that belongs to death is taken away from the person and he walks in the new life that belongs to the Son. While "we carry in our bodies the death of Jesus," we also reap the benefits "so that the life of Jesus may be revealed in our bodies" (2 Cor 4:10).

Sin after baptism.

The one who says "Our Father who art in heaven" but does not have the spirit of sonship is lying.

If you commit new sins, you are in a more evil state.

Yes, the one who presents himself for fornication after accepting the Holy Scriptures, his condemnation becomes greater than the one who commits adultery while under the law. It seems to me that there is a difference among those who have been baptized. There are some who have received the holy baptism, but then returned to subject themselves to the worries and pains of the world, drinking from the cup of salty desires.

www.ingramcontent.com/pod-product-compliance
Lightning Source LLC
Chambersburg PA
CBHW022005160426
43197CB00007B/276